Lucky 7

A COWMAN'S AUTOBIOGRAPHY

Lucky 7

A COWMAN'S AUTOBIOGRAPHY

By WILL TOM CARPENTER

Edited with an Introduction and Notes by
ELTON MILES

Illustrated by Lee Hart

AUSTIN : UNIVERSITY OF TEXAS PRESS

© *1957 by the University of Texas Press*

Library of Congress Catalog Card No. 57–7557

Manufactured in the United States of America

FOR

Walter Prescott Webb

WHO MADE THE WISH FOR IT

Contents

Introduction

WILL TOM CARPENTER's story of himself is a true Western romance of dusty and freezing work and a man's love of the freedom of the cattle trail. In vivid words Carpenter gives a clear picture of the struggle for life and fortune against half a continent of unfenced prairies that seduced a man and held him jealously. A land-locked plainsman, he cherished his "wide, wide world" of waving grass.

His story is romantic, because from the age of seven he loved the unfettered life of the cattle-driver, the labor of driving herds of longhorns across the free and flat grass-lands of Texas, Oklahoma, New Mexico, Kansas, Colorado, Montana, Nevada, Utah, and Arizona. One senses his feeling of power as he drove thousands of bellowing cattle before him, and his joyful independence as he moved them forward with almost limitless freedom of movement. Because of his freedom-loving spirit, he once ran away from home and eventually made his own spiritual and actual home on a saddle blanket. He is the Western Huckleberry Finn. Almost every description of his return to the trail is accompanied by a hymn of praise to the plains. He loved nature: his most beautiful memory was of the sun dogs in the winter of 1874–75, when he camped in a dugout to guard a herd of cattle on the blizzard-ridden prairies of eastern Colorado.

"No. 7"—as Carpenter[1] called himself—was raised in the West. He was born in Johnson County,[2] Missouri, on November 16, 1854, the youngest son of James and Cynthia Johnson Carpenter, and was taken as an infant by his family to Kansas before the Civil War. Since they were Southern sympathizers, the family feared violence and in 1862 took the Oregon Trail at Council Bluffs. They migrated with a wagon train up the Platte to the settlements near Pikes Peak. From that time forward, No. 7's story is the narrative of a boy who grew up to be a trail-driving cattleman, knowing little but the roving, horseback life of the free range.

This tale is also the story of a boy's growth to manly independence in a culture of no fixed habitation. Except for occasional desperate attempts by his brother and sister-in-law to teach him some book-learning on the ranch, Carpenter attended school only parts of three seasons. The schools in Missouri and at Fountain, Colorado, were built

[1] The only place in which a full name has been found for W. T. Carpenter is in the Terrell County death record for March 30, 1933. The informant was Carpenter's old friend and adjoining neighbor, Joe Kerr. Carpenter was called "Bill" and is still so referred to by those who knew him.

[2] *Sanderson Times,* March 31, 1933.

by farmers with permanent homesteads. No. 7's natural life was that of the rambling cowboy, who followed the grass and the market. Schools did not roll on wheels beside the chuck wagon.

No. 7's drives and trips make a catalogue of Homeric travels, for, like Ulysses, No. 7 was always seeking: 1862, from Council Bluffs up the Oregon Trail to Pikes Peak; 1864, from Monument Creek, Colorado, to Virginia City, Nevada, and Last Chance Gulch (now Helena), Montana; 1866, down the Missouri River by steamboat from Fort Benton, Montana, to St. Louis, and up the Mississippi River to Minnesota; 1867, from St. Louis along the Santa Fe Trail to Fountain Creek, Colorado; 1870, from Manitou Springs, Colorado, to Fort Laramie, Wyoming; 1871, down the Goodnight Trail from Manitou Springs to Red River Station (now Raton) and Carlsbad, New Mexico; 1872, from Manitou Springs to Abilene, Kansas, and Kit Carson, Colorado; 1876, from Colorado by iron horse to Denison, Texas, and by hack to Hempstead and Austin, then with a herd to Fort Griffin and Henrietta, Texas, in the short-grass country; 1882, from Abilene, Texas, to Odessa; 1883, his biggest cattle drive—12,000 head—up the Western Trail from Abilene, Texas, across the Red River at Doan's Store, through the Indian Territory, to Dodge City, Kansas; 1886, by rail to Bowie Station, Arizona, where he jumped the cattle out of the cars and drove them to Fort Apache; 1889, a sojourn on the XIT Ranch, with visits to Tascosa and Clarendon in the Texas Panhandle; 1890, a horse drive from Roswell, New Mexico, to Cheyenne, Wyoming; 1892, from Alpine, Texas, to the Pecos River.

Many of these drives started in Texas, where Carpenter lived after 1875. With his brother, J. B. Carpenter, he located on the Salt Fork of the Brazos River in Throckmorton County, in north Texas. In 1882 he formed a partnership in Jones County, in northwest central Texas, with William T. Hudson. Carpenter and Hudson claimed to have delivered the first corn-fed steers to be slaughtered in Fort Worth. In the early eighties, Carpenter moved to Bosque County, in central Texas, then spent several years in the Texas Panhandle managing trail herds and ranches, including the R. L. Elwood ranch in Donley County. In the spring of 1890, he moved the Elwood cattle to their new ranch south of Colorado City, in west Texas. The following year, he went back into the cattle business for himself in Sterling County, in west central Texas, forming a partnership with John S. McWilliams that lasted for three or four years. Carpenter then took charge of the Hereford Cattle Company and for the next three years managed their interests south of Alpine.[3] Soon this cattleman's Ulysses found his homeland—a free range west of the Pecos, where he herded his own cattle among the little hills of sparse dry grass and cactus until 1900.

In 1900 he settled permanently north of Dryden, built a house, fenced his land, and closed his own chapter in the romance of the Cattle Kingdom, after thirty-eight

[3] *The New Encyclopedia of Texas* (Texas Development Bureau, Dallas, n.d.), Vol. IV, p. 71. Apparently Carpenter was interviewed for the short biography contained in this book.

years of living the full life of the plainsman and cattle-trader of the West. The life he knew ended with the barbed-wire fence and the goat.

Carpenter was married in Missouri to Mattie Christenson, a native of Copenhagen, Denmark, where she was born on August 28, 1859.[4] They were married for more than fifty-years; they had no children. Until hard times struck during their old age, they lived in prosperity.

Not covered in his autobiography are Carpenter's last years. Just before World War I, he bought about twenty sections of land adjoining his ranch. In the brief depression that followed the war, unable to meet the payments due on the purchase, he gave up all but his home section. On that fenced-in one-mile square, lost in the endless prairies, he resigned himself to retirement.[5] After he lost his ranch, one of his most absorbing activities was the

[4] The exact marriage date of the Carpenters is not known. According to the *Sanderson Times* (September 4, 1936), Mattie Christenson's age upon her marriage to Carpenter was sixteen. *The New Encyclopedia of Texas* (Vol. IV, p. 71) states that they were married in Missouri. In his memoir, Carpenter states that late in 1875 and early in 1876, he was in Missouri enjoying the company of his pretty cousins and nieces and that he took the measles. In describing the events of 1882, Carpenter implies that he was married in that year. It seems most likely that Carpenter and Mattie Christenson were married in Missouri late in 1875 or early in 1876, just before Carpenter went to Texas with his brother. In his narrative, Carpenter does not discuss his own domestic life.

[5] Some light on Carpenter's later years may be shed by a letter from W. J. Bryan of Abilene, Texas, written on a Diamond T Ranch letterhead and postmarked February 11, 1931:

"Dear Bill. I notice where the gentleman from the 'Clear Fork' was taking Ft. Worth in. This looks funny, looks like we were destined to be old men 'by and by.' I am fighting this body but see some signs of old father time's ravage. I am sure the women notice it more. The ◇ caught Hell last winter, but things look good now. I hope to see you some day.   Bryan."

writing of this memoir. He died on March 30, 1933, in the Kerr Hotel at Sanderson, where he had gone for medical treatment.

Mrs. Carpenter survived her husband by three years and inherited his estate. She left no will and no living relative of hers could be found after her death on September 1, 1936, and the state of Texas became her heir. The property was disposed of through Louis Lemons, of Sanderson, the executor of her estate. The old house, in a run-down condition, still stands, twelve miles north of Dryden on the old Sheffield Road.

Carpenter stood about five feet, ten inches tall and weighed about one hundred and ninety pounds—all man. He wore a bristling mustache in his old age that was better kept in his younger days. It is said that he did not smoke or drink, though there is a photograph of him with a pipe in his mouth. He told friends that when he brought his herds to the end of the trail, in Abilene or Dodge City or some other rip-roaring cowtown, he let his men go on a spree but preferred to keep his money in his pocket and just walk around and see what was going on. This statement is in keeping with his personality as a writer, for a writer often observes more than he participates. Carpenter was a quiet man with little to say except to close friends.

Among other observations of Abilene and Dodge City Carpenter noted that often several herds would be grazing on the free grass just outside town, waiting for orders to come in to the railroad loading pens. The cowboys guarding the cattle did not let this prevent their trips into town. The second guard would go to town in the early part of the evening, and the first guard would go in after midnight, when the second guard came back to the prairie to go to work. In this fashion, they kept the town's night life going until sunup.

Carpenter remembered the section of Abilene known as McCoy's Addition as full of gambling halls, saloons, swindlers, variety shows, liquor, and women. The girls kept the boys dancing on a jitney-dance basis. After each dance the girl would take her partner to the bar. In payment for his dance, the boy would buy two very short beers at cutthroat prices. The girl received a check, which she would put in her stocking, and the fiddle would strike up again. The girl presented her checks at the bar the next morning and was paid her commission. Usually a fiddle was the only instrument in the dance hall because it was sufficient to dance to and was also less expensive than a piano or a band. Almost all the dancing was "round-dancing," as it was called, because it was quicker and the rounds of beer sold faster, making greater profits for bar and girls. There was very little square-dancing, for it took too long to finish a set.

Though there is some reference to McCoy's Addition in his autobiography, Carpenter was more interested in the everyday life and dealings of the cattleman. He loved his work and his position as owner or trail boss, and he loved to tell about them.

Mattie Carpenter has related how her husband, in retirement on his home section, would be seized with spells of restlessness. He would wander about the house and barn, besieged by memories that roved with ghostly cattle a thousand miles beyond his own barbed wire. Then he would head for his room, sit with his notebooks before him, and push his pencil slowly across the pages, re-creating the world that had disappeared before his eyes, in spite of his loving it so much.

Thus this book came to be written from the longing memory of a time-stranded cowman. It came into print as a result of a wish made by a historian.

In one of his talks about the Great Plains, in the fall of 1947, Walter Prescott Webb expressed a wish for a diary or a self-written account by an early Western cattleman who was more interested in his day-to-day work than in the Indian skirmishes that had happened nearby or the famous outlaws and marshals he had met. One of Professor Webb's listeners, I was momentarily transported to an imaginary trunk filled with yellowed receipts and bank statements, in which I would discover a handwritten sheaf of manuscript. I imagined deciphering penciled descriptions of communal roundups on the free range, cattle trades, long trail drives.

About a year and a half later, I moved to Alpine, Texas. Again it occurred to me that I might hear of such an account. If it existed anywhere, a likely place would be the Big Bend country. In the spring of 1950, after a class discussion in which I referred to Professor Webb's wish, a freshman student from Sanderson, Donald Smith, told me that his father had the manuscript autobiography of an old-time cattleman. Donald said that he and his father wanted to see something done with it and that he would like for me to look it over. In a week or two he brought me the manuscript.

If it does not fulfill all the requirements for the "dream book," it comes close to doing so. It consists of 185 numbered pages of boldly penciled manuscript without a title, written in great thrift on both sides from top to bottom and edge to edge. The first 42 pages are written on tablet letter paper and the rest in four brown "Boy Blue" composition books. The final page is a sheet of tablet letter paper, much frayed on the right-hand margin, where a few words are lost. Otherwise, the manuscript is complete. The composition books are numbered 2 to 4, and on the back of Number 3 is written in another hand:

Diary of
W. T. Carpenter—
His ranch is located 12
miles north of Dryden—

The "diary" proved to be an autobiography, apparently written, or at least finished, in the summer or fall of 1924.[6]

[6] Carpenter mentions certain events that seem to establish 1924, or perhaps 1925, as the year he finished his book. He alludes to Miriam A. Ferguson's campaign for the office of governor, which she assumed on January 20, 1925. The references to bobbed hair and the Ku Klux Klan, both of which flourished in the early twenties, strengthen this supposition.

As my regular duties allowed, I began making an exact copy of the manuscript, typing away at it as I could, letter for letter. This provided a working copy. Some time later a final, edited typescript was ready. I loaded the manuscript and the typescript in the car and drove with my fourteen-year-old son, Harry, through the mountain and range country from Alpine to Sanderson.

Sanderson is a ranching town in the mountains west of the Pecos. Like most small towns, it has one main street, which is also the main highway. Off Main Street are the maintenance shops of the Southern Pacific Railroad, serving the trains that cross the expanse of range lands between Del Rio and El Paso. In the opposite direction from Main Street is one of the best public schools in west Texas, a show place when it was first built. On a hill overlooking the town stand the most vital structures of any west Texas settlement, the water pumps and tanks. On the day we visited the town, green trees moved in the summer wind and Italian cypresses spired above the rooftops. Donald Smith was at home for a visit from California. On Main Street, in one of the store-window niches reserved for old-timers, sat his father, Chester Smith.

We went to Mr. Smith's little house, shaded by salt cedars, spread the manuscript on the kitchen table, and talked out the afternoon.

Chester Smith, sturdy, white-haired, with alert blue eyes, is one of Sanderson's earlier settlers, having come there in 1905. His interest in the lore of the cow country was aroused when he worked as an office boy for a San

Antonio cattle firm. As a youngster, he talked with Big-foot Wallace at the old International–Great Northern depot in San Antonio. He said, "Bigfoot was wearing that famous suit of his, made out of different animals: coon-skins, old possum hides, rabbits, and I don't know what all." One of his most thrilling boyhood memories is of finding a trunk in a barn, partly filled with letters and account records of an early cattleman. On rainy days he would read those accounts with great fascination. Now all those papers are lost. As a young man, he went to west Texas, where he worked as a cowboy, operated grocery stores in Dryden and Sanderson, and served as county commissioner of Terrell County for twelve years.

According to Mr. Smith, Lucky Seven's manuscript came to him from Carpenter's widow. Mr. and Mrs. Smith helped care for Mattie Carpenter in her last years. When Mr. Smith expressed interest in the manuscript, Mrs. Carpenter presented it to him out of gratitude. He has treasured it ever since and has arranged to have it deposited in the Sul Ross State College D.A.R. Texas-Southwest Library in Alpine.

At the kitchen table, Mr. Smith supplied much of the information on Carpenter's life that is not included in the memoir. Later, still talking about early times in the West, we visited the Carpenter graves in the Sanderson ceme-tery. When the sun started down behind the mountains, we bade each other goodbye.

My son and I sped home along the concrete highway, full of the day's talk about the old unfenced, longhorn-cattle kingdom, the thousand miles of unfenced pastures, and the jingling, lamplit cowtowns of earlier times. Now the pampered Hereford cattle gazed from behind their barbed-wire fencing, and a silver jet trail descended the sky to the horizon.

Will Tom Carpenter tells his story of those times and places in a most effective way, in the gritty language, the direct humor, the attachment to bald fact and frank opinion that characterize the Westerner. For example: "When we started out on the general round ups in the spring to gather our Cattle, which was a general mix up, we found ours the same as Everybody Else found theirs, (scattered from Hell to Breakfast). That was the time when a fellow had to sleep a-running." Another, summarizing the life cycle of the trail-driver: "I would sell a Bunch of fat steers in the fall to the beef buyers, and would go up into Mo. among the corn fed Girls and blow in, come back as soon or just a little before I got broke. Then I was good for another 12 months of hard work sleeping on wet saddle Blankets, working on round ups, line riding, laying out with the dry stock, etc."

The native style that Carpenter uses scholars might call "classical realism." He seems to select and relate certain bare facts that suggest much deeper truth lying beneath them. The restraint with which he tells his own unfortunate love story makes that narrative one of the most probing and ironic commentaries on human nature in biographical literature. And the relationship between trail-driving men and their women—and that third angle to the triangle, the Great Plains—is nowhere as strongly suggested as in Carpenter's account of the trail boss enduring the winter on the frozen plains when he might easily have gone home to spend the winter with his wife. But Carpenter tells this story with little comment or analysis. Between the lines are books of historical, economic, social, and domestic lore of the Cattle Kingdom and deep hints of the psychological effect of the free range on the mind of a growing boy and a mature man.

Carpenter was a natural writer, his style growing out of his spoken idiom. He had the rare instinct of conciseness in combination with a stock of hard-punching, emotional words. To illustrate: "About 3 weeks after they had started after those two widowed families, Brother stepped into the door and remarked to the surprised Bunch of us that father was dead." The diction as well as the narrative reveal Carpenter's appreciation of human experience, his awareness of the feelings of others, and, most important perhaps, his objectivity with regard to himself. That he had a sense of style is shown in the manuscript by the many insertions and frequent erasures and revisions, as he sought the right word or phrase. His sense of cliché and slang is often revealed by underlinings.

Though his spelling and punctuation are far from standard, Carpenter's sentence structure is sound and based on his spoken rhetoric. His mechanics also reflect the spoken language, for commas are used more for indication of pauses than for clarity, and underlinings are generally used for stress. After some study of the manuscript the difference between Carpenter's periods and commas becomes discernible, though at first glance they look very much alike. In editing, changes have been made that seem necessary for clarity and ease in reading. Chapter and paragraph divisions have been imposed, and overpunctuation has been reduced. Erroneously repeated words have been deleted, and in one instance the gender of a pronoun was corrected. The only additions to the original are the book title, the chapter titles, and four or five words inserted in an attempt to restore the final page.

Special gratitude is offered to Mr. and Mrs. Chester Smith and Donald Smith, of Sanderson, Texas. Thanks are also expressed to Mr. Ruel Adams, Mr. J. A. Gilbreath, Mr. L. H. Gilbreath, Mr. and Mrs. James Kerr, and Mr. Louis Lemons, all of Sanderson; Mr. Worth Frazer and Mr. Charlie Hunter, of Alpine, Texas; Professor Mody C. Boatright, of the University of Texas; Professors Dudley Dobie, Everett Turner, and John Prude and librarians Olive Blucher, Rose Kinzer, and LaNelle Skinner, all of Sul Ross State College, Alpine; and Mr. Larry Jones, gun hobbyist and Sul Ross student from Sweetwater, Texas.

To my wife, Lillian Neale Miles, I am grateful for her patience and encouragement.

ELTON MILES

Sul Ross State College
Alpine, Texas
January 15, 1957

Lucky 7

A COWMAN'S AUTOBIOGRAPHY

Rolling Our Dough

As I have found life in the wild & wooly west, among wild women, wild men, and everything else that might be called wild.

Me being the youngest one of a little family of seven, I'll just name myself No. 7 as there is nothing in a name anyway. All good sports and gamblers are rather parcial to no. 7 as it being a lucky card. I kinder think that way myself, for if it wasn't kinder lucky, I wouldn't be here to tell you about it now. I was borned in that famous old state where it is said that they all have to be showed. Well you can take it from me, if I hav'ent been showed, and several times at that.

My father moved over the line of Mo. into "bleeding Kan."[1] as it is called, when I was a small cub. And when

[1] During the Civil War, Kansas earned the name "bleeding Kansas" because of strife between northern sympathizers, called Jayhawkers, and southern sympathizers and slaveholders. Sometimes outlaws took advantage of the respective causes to commit crimes under the guise of patriotism.

the civil war, or rather the "uncivil" war come up, we moved to Colorado Ty. in 1862, for the Kan. Jayhawkers was making it most to hot for my Dad and two Bros. that I had. There was in our Family 3 Boys & 4 girls. The 2 oldest girls was married and both of their Husbands was in the southern army under Gen. Price.[2] The 2 youngest girls was just young girls about 12 and 14 years old. My bros. was about 22 & 24 years old. Well where we lived was right in the route where the Kan. Jayhawkers passed through the country, going on their Hellish rades, robbing, killing & burning Houses of southern sympathiers, hanging old men & boys, just raising Hell in general. You see your good union Neighbors would report you. When those Devils came through on their rades, we would leave our House at night and sleep in the woods, and well we did too.

In the spring of 1862 my Father thought the best thing we would do, would be to move camp. He had a little farm and about 150 head of cattle and some pretty horses. He was a Kentuckian, and all men from that part of the country liked good horses, so He had some of the old Ky. stock. He sold His little farm, and we all rolled our dough[3] for Colorado Ty, or rather Pike's Peak as all "Emigrants" called Colorado at that time.

As it has been so many years ago that I can't give the

[2] Sterling Price (1809–67), Brigadier General, United States Army, governor of Missouri, and Major General, Confederate States of America.

[3] Probably a figurative use of the expression for preparing sour dough for a journey. Biscuits were pinched off and baked for a quick meal on the trail.

exact names of the places that we passed through, only I know that we passed through Council Bluffs and traveled up the Plat River after stracking it. It was called Crossing the Plains at that time. Me & my youngest Sister rode on horse back and helped to drive the Cattle. That was my first job as a "Trail hand." We had two ox wagons. My oldest Brother was married, and He & His wife had a wagon with one yoke of oxon to it, and our family rode in the other wagon with two yoke of oxon hitched to it. There was another wagon or two along with families in them that was agoing to Pike's Peak also.

While traveling along up the Platt River, my Brothers wife taken sick. This was our first sorrow. We struck camp, and in about 7 or 8 days, she died. This was near a stage stand Called Kelly's Ranch, about 90 miles down on the Platt River below Denver. She was buried there, and we all swollowed our grief the best way we could and moved on towards the setting sun.

We moved on south of Denver about 35 or 40 miles. The Boys & my father builed a log cabin so as to live in through the cold winter. So along towards spring my father gave two horses to a man by the name of Spry for His ranch on the tip top of the divide, 40 miles south of Denver. This ranch consisted of one of the bigest and best pine log houses I have Ever seen before or since.[4] There

---

[4] In the first portion of his narrative Carpenter uses the term "ranch" in its early-day meaning of free range with buildings and small enclosures. In the latter part, dealing with later years, he generally uses the term in its current meaning—a bounded, titled area of land.

was a Barn built out of pine slabs and also about one half acre fenced in with big pine logs high enough to make a good corral, and all the land that you wanted to use as nobody owned any land there at that time. The nearest water was a creek called Plum Creek, with a very steep hill between the House & the Creek, which was to the best of my recollection about a quarter of a mile high. Well it most generally fell to No. 7's luck to carry the water. It certainly was a "Jonah" to me.

Some time in the spring of 1863 my father & oldest Brother started back to Mo. to get the two girls & their families and take care of them while their Husbands was fighting "the yanks." About 3 weeks after they had started after those two widowed families, Brother stepped into the door and remarked to the surprised Bunch of us, that father was dead. They had got as far as Omaha and father taken down with the flux and died.

So that fall my oldest Brother, as He was the leader of the family, taken all the cattle and moved them down south of the high divide country so they would winter better, taken them about 60 miles or near that on a creek called the Monument, near where the Beautiful City of Colorado Springs is today.

In the spring of 1864 we all got together all our belongings and started out on the road for Montana. During the fall of 1863 my uncle & His son, a boy about 20 years old, come out to us with a little bunch of cattle, about one hundred head. They were from Mo., near Lexington. The war got too warm for the old man, for He had one Boy in the Confederate Army under Gen. Price. So altogether we had about 300 cattle.

My older Brother, My Cousin, & myself was the cow boys. We didn't have to herd the cattle at nights, they all being gentle and no other cattle to mix with them. I rode one little red roan spanish mare all the way to Montana. My other Brother drove the wagon with two yoke of oxon hitched to it. The women folks rode in this wagon. My uncle had a wagon too and He drove it. We all had a pretty good trip, with the exceptions of having to cross all those rivers that lay between Montana & Colorado. Lots of them was swimming,[5] but there was ferry boats to cross the wagons on, but the cattle had to take the water. The 3 boys wasn't afraid of water, and they learned to take those rivers like they wasn't anything more than a spring Branch. There was one steer about 4 years old, white with a red head & neck, that led the herd all the way.

I remember that we layed over a couple of days, I think that it was some place in Wyoming, and the men folks went up in some mountains that was not over a few miles from the road and Killed a big Elk. They jerked the meat indian fashion so that it would keep until we could use it up. Some place along the road after leaving Denver, there was a couple more families joined our little crowd. They had a couple of wagons & a few head of cattle. They also come from where people had to be showed, so we were a very congenial bunch. There was 3 or 4 women & a young lady among our new friends. We always caught

[5] Too deep for fording.

7

plenty of trout, & fine ones too, when Ever we come to one of those mountain rivers. I remember, I think it was on Bear river,[6] that a Indian come to our Camp with about 10 or 12 big nice trout strung on a stick and gave them to us for a few bisquit. He had set on the Bank of the river and shot them with His arrows, as the water was very shalow & clear. This Indian, I will always remember how He looked. Oh, my! He was sure a big fine looking fellow. I think His tribe was what was called the Bloods,[7] and He looked every bit of it.

We had no Indian troubles those times that I even remember hearing of. We saw lots of Indians all along, but we had no fear of them. They were always wanting to trade for grub, calico, and such things that they didnt have themselves. But oh, my! they had to be watched when they were around camp, for they would steal anything that they could get off with. We passed Ft. Bridger and Ft. Fill Carny[8] on our way. There was quite a few soldiers and Indians too at those forts. There was quite a few what is called squaw men among the Indians in those days. Squaw man, means a white man with a Indian wife. The Government used them as interpeters.

In passing through Utah, we did not go very near Salt Lake City, but we passed through quite a Mormon settle-

[6] In northeastern Utah.
[7] A tribe closely related to the Blackfeet.
[8] Fort Bridger was in southwestern Wyoming, and Fort Phil Kearney was in northeast central Wyoming on the Bozeman Trail. (*Hammond's World Atlas* [Classics Edition], [C. S. Hammond & Co., Inc., New York, 1956], plates N-12, N-14.)

ment. The women would come out to our camps with all kinds of stuff to sell, such as eggs and vegetables. There was one fellow that was married to 3 sisters, and all three had red hair. I was too young then to know what danger that poor fellow was in; but since I have grown up, and learned a lot about red headed women, I have often wondered just how he come out of His matrimonial career. About fourth best would be my guess.

Well I guess that most all the western people have heard of the tough Boy from Bitter Creek. If you have every passed through that country and had to drink some of that water, you dont wonder at Him being tough. Believe me, it was something awful. You have heard the remark that some certain kind of bad whiskey would make a rabbit fight a bear. Well this water wouldn't make a rabbit fight a Bear—He might run over a Bear but wouldn't have him to stop for any fight, once he started on His way. It didn't make me run over any Bears, but I expect I would have run over one, if there had been one in my way.

Some time later in the fall we struck camp in the Galiton valley on the Galiton River, about 100 miles from Virginia City then the capitol of the Territory.[9] So the two Brothers cut logs and builed a cabbin, dobbed the cracks with mud, and covered the top with dirt. It dont rain in that northwestern country in the winter, but you can take it from me that it snows. There was a world of

[9] Virginia City, about sixty miles southeast of Butte, was the capital of Montana Territory from 1865 to 1875 and a gold-mining center.

wild game, from a cotton tail rabbit to a Grizzly Bear, so we feasted on all Kinds of wild game. My two Brothers being Extra good hunters, as well as fine shots, about Xmas they Killed a load of game and hauled it to Virginia City, sold it, and brought back a lot of supplies.

We had a few neighbors living around not far off, so it didn't seem so lonely. There was a couple of fellows that spent the bigest part of the winter with us. They were also from that state where they have to be showed, in fact they were about thirty-second cousin of ours. They had drifted out there to dig up some of those big nuggets that they had been reading about. Well they all had a better time that winter than I had, because there wasn't room around the card table of nights for a kid like me, but they saw that I was intertained by bringing in wood & keeping a good fire. They also danced on the old dirt floor, for there was a fiddler, & a good fiddler, in the camp.

The winter was going by pretty nice, until our Darling old Mother taken sick with the pneumonia and died. Then our grief come back to us once more.

Well as I have said that we had some neighbors, so we did, and one of them, a man about 27 years old, that had a Ranch about 5 miles from our Place, married my oldest sister, and they moved to Virginia City to live and taken my other sister along. That left us 3 boys. So when spring opened up we started to go to a mineing town called Grizzly Gulch, now called Helena, the capital of Montana,[10] & my brother driving the ox wagon, & my

10 Gold was discovered by John Cowan in the valley of the Prickly

oldest brother & I driving the cattle. As near as I can remember there was about 250 head or over.

We was quite a while making this little drive, for the winter broke out again, and we had to go into camp for a while. When we left the Mo. river one morning and started across a high divide, we had to go about 12 miles across to the next creek. The wagon allways went in the lead of the cattle, and that old red headed steer would follow that wagon just the same as a calf would follow its mama. No matter where it went, if He could go, He would, so it always made it easy on us to drive the cattle. I was still on the Haricane deck of my old roan mare. Perhaps you would like to Know Her name—well it was just plain old Beck, and Beck carried me many a mile.

When we got about half way across this divide, it began to rain, and we all had on Buckskin clothes out & out,[11] except our hats & shoes. It rained until we got our buckskins good & wet, if you know what a wet Buck skin means. Then it quit raining and began to snow. Well our cattle faced the music & we had to.

When we got to the creek there was quite a good bottom covered with timber, mostly cotton wood, and the snow by that time was about 3 inches deep. We found a family camped there had a wagon, an old pair of ponies and no shelter for the family. There was a woman, two

---

Pear River in 1864, and the stake was called Last Chance Gulch. Here Helena was founded and named in October of the same year. (*The Works of Hubert Howe Bancroft* [The History Company, Publishers, San Francisco, 1890], Vol. XXXI, p. 721.)

[11] That is, wore nothing but buckskin.

little boys, about 4 & 6 years of age, and a Husband with the Consumtion. We turned all our stock loose in the Bottom, cut down some cotton wood trees so the horses could get the Bark to Eat, then went to work and fixed a kind of shelter with wagon sheet & Bresh. We all got under it and dried our clothes. If you never wore any Buckskin clothes and was caught out in such a prediciment, you cant eppreciate what I am telling.

Well the storm lasted about 3 days, and when it cleared off, the snow was about 12 inches deep. When the boys got out to look after the stock, they found that we had about 20 head of cattle, one yoke of oxon, and our horses. The balance of the cattle had drifted back to where we had started from 3 days before, so we gathered up what we had left and back trailed after the cattle. We found them alright and happy, for it had not snowed a bit back there where the cattle was. It was a place that was called Hot Springs a few miles from the Mo. River,[12] so we thought that we would hold up there until the weather got warmer, or until we was certain that the snow was over. I dont Know what month this storm was in, but I think it was in the latter part of April 1865.

Well then we had some more troubles. It was our Bellies this time—no grub in the country to be had for love, money or chin music. This shortage of grub was caused by a heavy snow storm stracking in between Ft. Benton & Grizzley Gulch, a distance being about 200 miles. Ft. Benton was the head of navigation on the Mo. river and all supplies for the Territory was freighted in from there, either by mules or Bull teams, and on account of the deep snow, the teams had to lay up and wait for the snow to melt off, so that they could travel. There being more people in the Territory than grub, the people soon

[12] Hot Spring, Montana, stood about where Jackson stands today, on the Big Hole River, which flows into the Jefferson River (a fork of the Missouri) about fifty-three miles to the east. The Missouri forms about ninety-five miles northeast of where Hot Spring was situated. (*People's Popular Atlas of the World* [Thompson & Thomas, Chicago, 1903], p. 125.)

won the victory by eating up the grub. For six weeks longer there was not a dust of flour in the whole Territory of Montana.

In a short time we broke camp and moved our little hungry outfit within 7 miles of the Big gold mineing Town called Grizzley Gulch, now the nice city of Helena. We camped on a nice mountain stream by the name of Prickly Pare, and it shure did have the right name, for if there had been any more room for the pesty stuff to have grown, I am sure that there would have been more pare. There was pare on top of pare and then some. This pare only covered a valley about a half mile in width. The grass was certainly fine, as it had hardly even been bit, only by some wild animal. It was only about 2½ or 3 miles up to the mountains where this beautiful stream come down from.

There was an old deserted pine log cabin where we struck camp. There was about 4 men below our camp on the creek, trying to mine. They had a Big hole dug, but the water come in on them so fast that it kept them busy bailing the water out. I used to go and watch them work, as it wasn't but a few hundred yards from our Camp. They all seemed to be good fellows, and they all liked to talk to me, being that I was a pretty nice Boy at "that particular time," for I had been grown up under a Bush, or part of one, say for instance one of the *branches*, a foot or so long. Well you know boys who knew just how heavy those kind of little timbers felt when they happen to be in the way when they fell, was pretty good Boys. My

14

oldest Brother was very severe when aroused too high above zero.

The boys got a contract that summer to furnish some of the Butchers beef in the mining Town. Being only 7 miles, they drove in 6 or 8 head of fat cattle most ever day. They got .18¢ a pound on foot in gold dust, and settled up every Sat. night. Being no Banks in the Place, they brought the money home with them in Buckskin sacks ranging in length from 5 inches to 8 or 10. So they hid it around in the Camp in old oyster cans and such other things as they saw fit. No one knowing that they brought money to Camp, it was pretty safe.

Well with all that yellow stuff hid around, we was hungry. The boys nearly always brought back some fine fat beef steak, but we had no salt, no bread, and little of anything else, only dried grapes, dried peaches, and milk. You can just imagine how fat the beef was after living on that fine Montana grass, which had never been bitten before by a cow. Me being just a kid, it went pretty tough with me. I couldn't eat the fat beef, for you can imagine how flat and gaggy it tasted to a kid, when it didn't even have salt to put on it. So I ate dried peaches and milk, when the Boys had time or taken the pains to drive up the old cow that we milked. And when they didn't No. 7 just ate a few dried peaches and swelled up a little. For the rest that I would have been thankful for, was "shy on the menu." The Boys seemed to stand the drouth pretty well, but No. 7 felt & looked like He was playing the duce against the whole deck.

When the snow did melt away so that the freighters could bring their supplies to the Town, the merchants was very careful to rashion out the flour so that it would go round. If there was 3 or 4 in a family or Camp, they would sell you 6 or 7 lbs. at $1.50 a lb., so no one asked the merchant to be played as a favorite. But as the freight came into the country more readily the price came down a lot. But still you knew that you had bought something when ever you had to build up your commissary.

I remember when our flour began to get close to the bottom of the sack. I mean the upper end of the flour getting close to the lower end. That was the commencement of the situation that we wouldn't make bread of the flour, but use it by making what is called thicken milk. We would put the milk in a pot, set it on the fire, & when it come to a boil, then stur in some flour, just wet enough to be kinder sticky & stringy. We sure did make the last few lbs. of flour last a long time, for we knew the impossible. But as the old saying is that there never was a purse so long but what it had an end. Well that applies to a flour sack as well as purses. So we finally found the end of that much dearly beloved flour sack, but before that snow melted off, No. 7 began to think that it was "loaded & fired."

The summer being over, and the cattle being all butchered out, we went back to the Galiton valley on a little visit to see our Sister that had married early in the spring. She & Her Husband had moved back to the Ranch & farm from Virginia City. The other sister had married

16

while in Virginia City and stayed there, so I never have seen Her since, but she is still living in the far Northwest and ought to be enjoying life, as Her Husband was a mining man and left Her plenty of money when He died, which was about 20 years ago. She is about 4 years older than I, but she is young for Her years & jolly, for I get letters from Her sometimes, when she can spare the time to write.

She sent me Her picture about 2 years ago, and she looked to be about 35 or 40 and pretty, standing beside Her big fine Car, with a big seal skin coat on. She didnt look like the gal that went to Montana in a prairie schooner in 1864. For over 30 years she thought I was dead, because she never heard from me after I sacked my saddle and boarded the M. K. & T. R-R-[13] to ride it as far as it run south and promised myself that walking wasn't all taken up. That all happened in 1875. So after so many years, I thought I would see if I was detective enough to find Her. I wrote to all the places, where I knew she had once lived and would find that she had left there and went to some other place. But I camped on the old girls trail and found Her living in the "Grand City of Seven Hills" (Seattle). I will not write any more on this subject, but I could keep on writing about Her, as I still think of Her as my Sister & play mate.

Now I will go back from this incident a few years and give an account of the happenings before making the visit to the Galiton valley. When we got rid of the cattle, we

[13] The Missouri, Kansas, and Texas Railroad (the "Katy").

moved away from Prickly Pare creek, taking our horses with us. We struck camp at or near a stage stand called Spokcane. A young fellow and His sister was keeping a eating House there. So it was there that my oldest Brother (the widower) found His "water lou."

Well after the Boys stayed a few days visiting our sister, they went back towards Helena and left me with my sister. They bought a herd of 400 Calif. Cows that had been driven in from there by a man by the name of Maj. Bradley (afterwards got to be Gov. of Nevada).[14] So the boys started a little ranch on the Mo. River about 26 miles from Helena. There the oldest Brother went and got his "water lou" and give Her the job as Ranch keeper. Then some time during the winter, my other Brother came to my sisters after me. This was in the winter of 1865 & 66. That was the last time that I ever saw Her. She died about 3 years ago, near Butte, Montana.

So after riding hard for two days, we landed at the Ranch safe but not altogether sound, for I was shy about a dollars worth of skin, for the Horse that He brought me wasn't old Beck. He was so darn rough that on that trip I first began to shed my puppy teeth.

Right here No. 7 was played against the queen & duce too, "ie" I thought I had played the duce after I began to learn the winning ways of my new red headed Irish sister in law west of the Rockies (Not the law west of the Pecos). Well sir, she was really the sweetest liear that I

<hr>

[14] Lewis R. Bradley, born in 1835, was elected governor of Nevada in 1870. (*The Works of Hubert Howe Bancroft*, Vol. XXV, pp. 190, 194.)

had ever got up against. Right here I commenced to learn something that I didn't want to learn, about red headed women. My Brother got it into His head that I must study my Book (and it was right too) so she was to see that I did. Well she always found something for me to do as soon as the boys was out of sight. And when my Brother would return at night, He would call me up to hear my lesson that had been marked for me the night before, and of course I hardly ever knew a blooming bit of it.— And she would tell Him, that I wouldn't mind Her and that she couldn't get the "young sauce Box" to look at His Book after they had got out of sight. Right then the war paint would show up, bright and plenty.

19

I had sense enough, even if I was a Kid, to not dispute Her word, for I suppose all Bride's words are looked on as being Holy, sweet & truthful, as long as they are "Honey mooning." I saw that No. 7 was being played against the queen with big odds, so I stood right up to the mouth of the Gun, like a good soldier, that I was. You have often heard Boys say that they wished to be a man. Well I wished to be a Grizzly Bear, as that was the most ferocious thing that I could think of, for I didnt think that just being a man would win any championship over a red headed Irish Biddy that tipped the scales at about 185 lbs.

I felt by this little unhappy period of my young & growing life like I did about the snow melting off, that I was growing up slowly and would be over the danger line some day if I could only hold out that long. And to the happiest moment of my life, I did, so No. 7 proved to be the wining card in the End. But by that time, she sure was proving Herself master of the situation. As I growled *out*, Brother growled *in*, and His water lou proved true to the name.

I often think that I was gamer than my Big Brother, for I allways stood right up to the "mouth of the Gun," while He had to stand "attention." So after 10 years wearing a "green Badge," He left it off and pinned on the Yellow Rose of Tex. But I am getting ahead of my story, only I hated to wring off this last subjeck after getting once started out on it.

That winter, after buying the 400 head of Calif. cows, they marketed those cows at Helena that winter by driving in 15 or 20 at a time. So by Spring they had a small bunch left, about 30 head I think, and they had some mighty good horses that they brought with the cows. My other brother got married that spring, about a week before My Brother & his wife & I left for the states. I never got to see my new sister as I wasnt being considered among so many Brides. So the Boys divided there gold, and my Brother that had just married Kept the Ranch, saddle horses, and the reminant of Cattle.[15] It was in June 1866 He went into Helena with us, and I never saw Him again. He has been dead over 35 years.

Well we got aboard a four mule wagon and struck for Ft. Benton a distance of 200 miles. It taken about three days and a half to make the trip. There we found an old sturn wheeler by the name of the Huntsville laying there ready to start down the River for St. Louis. There was the first steam Boat I ever saw.

Just before the boat was ready to start, some men drove a big fat gentle ox up near the boat, and they put a big rope around his horns and fastened the other end of the rope to what was called their spar pole, and swung him clear of the ground about 25 feet in the air and let him down on the lower deck. He never moved after being let down. I suppose that the weight must have broke his neck, as he must have weighed 12 or 15 hundred pounds. Then he was butchered.

[15] Cattle still scattered after the roundup is over, or cattle strayed from the herd on a drive and left behind. The remnant is not considered to be abandoned by the owner.

Going down the river there was lots of very interesting things to see, being that the Boat did all its traveling in the day time. It tied up of nights, until it got quite a long ways down the river, on account of the river being very high, crooked & snaggy. I remember one day going along pretty fast as the river is very swift, that a man was setting on the edge of the lower deck fishing. The Boat hit the Bank, and off he went in the river. Of Course the Boat was going Fast, it left Him behind right now. I never will forget how that poor cuss hollowed, Bring the yawl, bring the yawl, bring the yawl. They let down a small boat that was swung up to the side of the Boat and taken Him in.

All along down the river there was worlds of Buffalo to be seen, and Indians too. We passed lots of big Indian villeages. We passed a Gov. Fort or two,[16] quite a long ways down the river from Ft. Benton. The Boat always stopped at these forts. There was lots of Indians come near the Boat at those places, to look and to buy. I remember seeing people that was on the Boat throw things in the river, such as bread, crackers, etc., just to see the little naked Indian boys jump in the river after it. Some little Devils which looked to be not over 6 or 7 years old, would jump in where it must have 15 or 20 feet deep, swim like

[16] Fort Union was situated on the Missouri River in Montana, a few miles west of the present North Dakota line, in the Fort Union Military Reservation. Fort Clark and Fort Mandan were situated on the Missouri below the mouth of the Yellowstone River. (*Historical Atlas of the United States* [Henry Holt and Company, Inc., New York, 1953], p. 44; *People's Popular Atlas of the World*, p. 125.)

a duck. I also saw at one of those forts, where the Boat had stopped, two Indian men cross over to our side in a round raw hide Boat, just big enough for them to set in. And when they landed, one picked up the Boat and carried it off on His head.

The river was very high too, and swift. The Buffalo and Indians neither fear water. I seen lots of Buffalo swimming the river. One day there was a big old buffalo swimming the river, and the man at the wheel had to turn His Boat a little to keep from running over him. Some fellows got a rope and tried to get it on the Bulls head, but didn't succeed. The quick sand was pretty bad in the river, and we saw lots of buffalo go in and sink almost out of sight. Just could see the top of their hump & horns, and I guess they soon went out of sight entirely. They didn't seem to care for seeing the Boat, at least they wasn't scared of it.

One day when we passed a big Indian village, about 20 Indians on horse back run after the Boat until their horses looked to be playing out. Some thought that they wanted to shoot into the Boat, but the river was pretty wide, and the Boat kept out pretty well to the opposite side to where the Indians was.

There was no wood yards along the river until we got quite a ways down. So every day the Boat would tie up for an hour or so, and the Deck hands would go ashore, cut wood, carry it onto the Boat.

When we passed Omaha, I saw my first R-R- Cars. I think we was 15 days getting to St. Louis. There I saw my first big city. By that time I was kinder getting used to civilizedation, so we there taken a steamer, (I think its name was the Dimond Joe) up the Miss. River, headed for Minn. That was where my red headed sister in laws Folks lived, for of Course she had to show the old Folks what she had caught in the wild & wooly west.

Some Place up the river, where we quit the Boat and was to take the Train, my Brother got left. So we went on to some Place, I dont know the name of it, and stopped, and Brother taken a Boat and caught us. We had all the money, above $6,000.00 in gold dust, had it in a little hand Bag. It was heavy too. Well we both set over that hand Bag like a Chilled Kitten would set over a warm Brick. He certainly was glad to get back to us & His "dough." I dont know at this time why He didn't leave it in the Bank at St. Louis, but He didn't, and that is all I know about it.

We finally landed at the Home of my red headed sister's happy child hood, was treated all right by the old Folks. They had a pretty good little farm and lived pretty well, as all farmers do that own their own farms. After being there near a month, Brother & I was agoing down into Mo. where our two sisters lived; and my red headed sister was agoing to stay with Her mama & papa and finish out Her visit. We got as far as Lacross, Wis., and we found that the Cholera was rageing down about St. Louis, so we doubled back to Minn. again. We stayed there until late in the fall, until the Cholera scare was over, then we all three started for Mo. and we got there alright this time without any delays.

That was the first time that I every remember of seeing my two oldest sisters. Of Coarse I had seen them, but too young to remember them. Just think! one had two Boys that was older than I was. Well my two Sisters lived about 3 miles apart so I visited with Both of them that fall until school started, or until *I* started.

Then No. 7's troubles all come again, worse than Ever. The school house was builed out of logs, and well it was, for if I had a thought I had any chance to have broke out, I think that I would of "led a stampede," and if you could realize how scared I was, you would still be wondering why I didn't. The Teacher was an old Neighbor Hood quack Doctor, about 82 or 83 years old, His head as white as 80 years could make it, and He had a big mole on the side of His nose, but oh, my! wasn't He the yellow Tom cat's goat tee. He used to make young ladies 16 & 17 years old stand in the middle of the floor and whip them with a swich, and Boys that was just as big as they ever got to be, taken the same treatment.

One day I was setting on my Bench, (that was what we had to set on) and He called me by name. I looked up, just as scared as a march hare, and He said, Come here to me.

Right then I was sorry that the House was builed out of those big logs. I never did run from fear before or since, but you can take it from me, that I sure did feel like leading a stampede. So I walked right up in the mouth of the gun, for I knew it was loaded (son of agun) and stood at attention.

He sure did give me the right & left hook, on Both sides of my face good and hard, believe me; then said, Go back to your seat sir.

Could anyone blame a poor Kid, that had been living all His life (to the age of 12) among men, in the west, for being scared stiff.

Well he rode an old poor gray horse or mare, I don't know which; but I do know that I went His way about a quarter of a mile & the road led into a lane, and there was a gate that He always made me open for Him. He always seen that I started on ahead in plenty of time. It is one of my past time pleasures at this present day and time, and has been every since, to think of that old Demon, and hate Him with all the hate that could possible be in any one heart.

I had to walk 2½ miles & coon a foot log. If you have ever cooned a log for about 50 feet cold icey mornings in one of those northern states, you would be sorry.—I often thought of, and wished for old Beck, my old roan spanish pony, but—a las! Well those times was real school days, when a fellow needed a friend.

When kids went to those log cabin colleges, if they didn't have head lise, they had worse, the itch, and some had both. So after going about a month or six weeks, I caught the itch. The right name is the 7 year itch, so I layed off to get rid of it. I was greased with lard & sulphor

until you could smell me as far as you could smell a Billy goat in the fall of the year, if you know what that means.

Well I didnt go back to finish my education any more that winter. I liked all the Boys and girls that went to the school for they was nice to me, and I would tell them a lot of things about the west that interested them.

In spring my Brother began to talk about buying up a little herd of ma yearlings and driving them back to Colorado. This was the spring of 1867. My sister wanted my Brother to leave me with them so that I could learn to "work," and go to school, (work mostly). Of course He had no notion of doing it, but He asked me if I wanted to stay, I suppose just to hear what I would say. I said I *wouldn't* stay, before He got the words out of His mouth.

When He told them I wouldn't stay and that He didn't feel like making me stay, one of them, (the oldest) spoke up and said, Well if I was hung for stealing horses, it would be no fault of Hers. So I didn't stay, and I haven't been hung for stealing horses yet.

My Brother bought up a little herd of yearlings, about 200 head and loaned our Cousin, that come to us in 1863, money enough to buy 50 head, so we started out from Lexington, back to Colorado. My red headed sister was along, good & strong, for she had wintered well on hog and hominy. A Brother to our Cousin went along and drove the wagon with one yoke of oxon hitched to it. He was the one that was in the confedderate army during the war, and there was still another fellow along that helped drive the cattle. So there was four of us with the cattle.

My Brother had a two horse Hack that His wife drove, and they also slept in it.

We got along pretty well for quite a distance. In the mean time there had been several families fell in with us that was going to Colorado also, and there was a mexican train which consisted of about 15 teams, about 9 or 10 yoke of oxon to the team, hitched to two wagons, one being trailed behind the other, and loaded with all Kinds of supplies for Santafee, N.M.

One Evening we was all travelling along pretty nice, the herd behind the whole outfit, and those wagons that had the families in them was in the back of the mexican trains. But our two wagons was behind all the other wagons, and just ahead of the little herd. We was just coming into a good big Bottom, and there was a creek (called Cow Creek) just ahead and it had some timber on it. The lead wagons was getting pretty close to this creek and riding along behind the cattle.

My Brother made the remark that this was a pretty good place for red skins, (meaning Indians). He had went from Levenworth to Salt Lake City with a Bull Train, and walked and drove one of those big Bull teams all the way there & back in 1859, so He had a pretty good idea of the west.

Well it wasn't more than 15 or 20 minutes after He made the remark about the red skins, until we heard the shooting coming off, and seeing those wagons that was ahead of the main train, running back toward the Train and the Indians was after them on horse back. And you

can take it from me that there wasn't any jockeying going on either. There was one wagon from Arkansas and it had two yoke of cherikee steers[17] hitched to it. Talk about running, they made it back to the train in "nothing flat."

There was a dutchman traveling with that wagon. He was walking along with the driver when the Indians got after them. They killed him and scalped him. The driver had an old Brindle rifle,[18] and the Indians did not

[17] "In eastern Texas, the Cherokee Indians had a special breed of cattle that they were forced to abandon when they were driven from the land. For years some of them propagated mustang stock." (J. Frank Dobie, *The Longhorns* [Little, Brown & Company, Boston, 1941], p. 32.) Cherokee cattle were Spanish longhorn cattle that came into the United States through Florida and moved westward with the Cherokee migrations.

[18] A Kentucky rifle with the early type of full-length, curly-maple

get close enough to Kill Him. He ran along the side of His team. They cut off the lead wagon when it crossed the creek. It belonged to a Kansas City man by the name of Divers, or some such a name. It had two big Mo. mules and hitched to a new wagon loaded with can goods. They killed the old man, which was about 45, scalped Him, taken the most of His clothes off of Him, and left His axe sticking in His back, cut His Harness up, burned His wagon and taken his mules. Believe me, business "picked up" around that little Bunch of travelers pretty fast & plenty.

We moved on after we saw that the Indians had gone. It was all done quick.

We had another creek to cross just like the first one, by the same name, one Big Cow Creek and the other Little Cow Creek. But the outfit used precaution after we had that scare, so that there was about 4 of the men went back that night and buried the two dead men.

Well we moved on until we got to Ft. Dodge, which was I think about 2 days travel, and there the Government held us up until there was some more wagons come along & joined us. The Captain at the Fort made my Brother Captain of the whole Train. We did not get run into any more, but my Brother kept scouts out every day. The Indians Killed a stage driver about 50 miles ahead of us. You see the stage run from Ft. Dodge, Kansas, to Ft. Lion, Colorado, a distance of 200 miles, but I think

stock. The design of the stock is credited to W. P. Brindel, late-eighteenth-century gunsmith of eastern Kentucky.

perhaps that the stage swung out by Ft. Hays, as I dont remember of ever seeing any stage stands up the Arkansas river, but I am not quite so certain about it.[19]

After we left Ft. Dodge, we only had one little scare, and that was when about two of our scouts that was on ahead about a mile, saw a bunch of soldiers, about 12 or 15, coming down the River towards them. The two scouts thought that the soldiers was Indians, and the soldiers thought the same about the two scouts, so the scare was on. We seen a hell of a dust coming down the road, and it was coming fast, believe me. Then we saw the two men, and the soldiers behind bringing up the rear so darn fast, that it looked for a while like there wasnt going to be any rear. Of course the soldiers was quite a little distance behind and when they did show up, on top of a little rise in the road about 200 yards from the Train.

They found the wagons all corraled in propper shape, and the men all behind their wagons, (them that wasn't under them) with their guns ready for "target practice." When each party saw their mistake, they all felt good and had a big laugh, only I think some of them was scared so darn bad that they couldn't even raise a grin.

I guess you might be wondering what No. 7 was doing

[19] The Butterfield stagecoach route followed the Arkansas River from Fort Dodge, Kansas, to Fort Lyon and Bent's Fort, both in southeastern Colorado. Fort Hayes was situated down the river from Fort Dodge, about where Great Bend now stands. (Roscoe P. Conkling and Margaret B. Conkling, *The Butterfield Overland Mail* [Arthur H. Clark Company, Glendale, Calif., 1947], Vol. III, *Atlas,* sheet I; Ralph Henry Gabriel (ed.), *The Pageant of America* [Yale University Press, New Haven, Conn., 1929], Vol. II, p. 203, map.)

all that time. Well I guess that I showed just about as much nerve as any of them, for I had crawled in the Hack, where my red headed Irish sister in law was.

After that things went alright, but there wasn't barely a day that we didn't see Indians way off on some of the Hills.

After getting up into Colorado, the outfit began to split up and each fellow going to where He had started to. We moved up Northwest of Pueblo about 35 miles on a creek called Turkey creek, it was near the mountains, struck camp for the winter, or rather taken up a little place for a ranch. Had a few neighbors, but not close enough for the chickens to mix, if there had been any chickens, which there wasn't. My Brother taken His wife to Denver that fall and Boarded Her with some friends that we used to Know in Montana by the name of Slone.

Now right here is where No. 7 is going to tell you some more of his troubles.

Right Up with the Best

TO GET AT IT RIGHT, I will first tell you that my Brother's first wife's people had moved to Calif. during the time that we was all tromping around, and Brother had never seen them after we all started to Colorado in 1862, so He still had Her Trunk, (I mean His dead wife's) and it had all Her belongings. God only knows How the fellow Kept that Trunk all the time while traveling around but He did all the same, so after leaving His wife in Denver, He came back to the Camp, and He left our cousin in charge of the little outfit. He told us that He was agoing to Calif. to see His dead wife's People and take that Trunk along and give it to Her mother.

He told my cousin that when the school started up

over on the Fountain, (that was a creek East of us about 15 miles, which was being farmed by quite a lot of People) to take me over there and get a place for me to board and leave me there to go to school. Me being crazy about camp life, riding a pony, being with the men, etc., you can imagine just how I felt when I heard those orders. And I had got to be a pretty good little hunter and there was all Kind of game, so I saw I was up against the real thing again, for I hadn't forgotten my first school in Mo. I thought that all Teachers was alike, but I knew that I had to go and made up my mind to take my medicine if it was bitter.

So when school started, my cousin taken me over there and got a nice place for me to stay at a farmers by the Name of White. He had a lovely wife & one little Boy about 4 years old. The lady was awful nice to me, but Holy Cats, it was 5 miles to the school House and poor me had to walk. What would you think *that* meant to a Kid about 13 years old.

Well sir the first day I taken my lunch and hiked out down the Road to school. Got along all right, had quite a different teacher to what my old Dr. was. I liked the few scholars that was there, which was about 6 or 7. There was one good big Girl, I guess which she was about 16 years of age. She taken a fancy to me and was awful nice to me. I still remember that Her name was Kate Banester. Dont remember any of the Boys names now, for they was just only Boys, but I always did have quite a *habit* of re-membering *Girls*.

That first night I made it back to my Boarding House after supper. I wasnt very long in "hitting the hay."

So next morning I cranked up and struck out in high. After getting to the school House, I found that there wouldn't be any school for a week. Back I went and I made it by about noon, and I got togather my ward Robe, which couldn't have been very much for I was standing in nearly all of it at the time. I told The Folks that I was going to camp that Evening, a distance of 15 miles. I had walked 10 already, so I said "au revoir" and high tailed it for camp. There was not a soul living near my Road nor a drop of water, but about sundown I parked my carcass at Camp. I didn't go back again after anymore "learning."

So after I got over my soreness from the long walk, I had a pretty good time until Brother came back from Calif., which was about 2 months. Then no. 7 had some more trouble.

He taken me over on the creek about 15 miles farther up and started me to another log cabin college. Got me a pretty good Place to board at a farm House. It was only about one mile from the school House. The People had one Boy about 5 years old and a little Girl (a Niece) about 8 years old, and a smart little girl she was too, when it come to Books. But Oh, hot tomollies! how that woman used to whip those two Kids. She whipped with a keen switch, if that means anything to you, but she didn't show any parshality.

The Teacher was a man. Guess He didnt know very

much, for He Kept them all in their old Blue Back spelling Book. You had to go clear through it before He would let them study anything Else, but I dont think any of them ever got to "Daniel Webster's rear."[1]

There was one little incident that I never will forget, that happened at that little Log Cabin College. One Evening I had committed some Kind of Crime which wasn't quite punishable by death, but I dont know now just what I was found guilty of. But I had to stand up on one of the Benches. While I was standing up on that Bench, I could see out of the window quite a ways up the road, and what do you suppose I saw? Well sir I had rather of seen anything that I had ever seen before or since than to have seen what I did see. It was my Brother & His wife coming from Denver in their white topped Hack, working a gray mule & a red roan one, so there could be no mistake in their idenity. Just imagine how this poor Kid felt thinking that they would come straight to the school house. I believe that I would of "rattled my hocks"[2] if they hadnt a stopped at a house just when they did, so they didnt come to the school House atal.

I stayed the school out, which I guess was about two months. Then I returned to Camp, or the Ranch you might call it, for Brother had builed a House. I got through the summer pretty well, nothing going very bad. When fall came, my troubles began again (more school

[1] The back pages of the *Blue Back Speller*—Noah Webster's *An American Spelling Book.*

[2] A bovine's hocks knock together when it runs or gallops.

days). I think that cartoon of the ragged Boy, where it says when a fellow needs a friend, is the "real cooky."[3]

Well there was an old hard shell Babtist Preacher that lived 4 miles up the creek above where we lived, by the name of old Tomy Rule. His son was married to His wife's sister. They had a few cattle and a little ranch. There was 2 or 3 Kids in the Family, so they had a man to teach them. He was a big fellow about 30 years old, had red hair and long red whiskers, not exactly the Tom cats whiskers, but just plain red whiskers. He was what is called clubed footed. His feet was as round as a foot Ball. Sure did look funny to see Him walk on those two "feet Balls," put one right over the other Every step He taken.

I went a week to that College, walked 4 miles & back Every day. I never Can understand now, when I get to thinking about my school days, why they made me walk. There was plenty of ponies on the Ranch.

The one week ended that year's schooling, so the next spring we got togather our little outfit and moved north onto Cherry Creek about 15 miles South of Denver. There we builed a little House, corrals etc., and spent the summer. In the fall we moved back to the Fountain again, about 40 miles south of where Colorado Springs is now builed.

So the next spring we got our outfit togather & started to Montana, and we got as far North as the Laramie River in Wyo. 24 miles above Ft. Laramie and sold out

[3] "When a Feller Needs a Friend" was a syndicated newspaper cartoon popular in the 1920's drawn by Clare Briggs.

to some ranch men that lived there by the Name of Cra-ton & Hutton. Then we all pulled back to Denver. My cousin left us there & went back to Mo. Then Brother, His wife & I went down to the Fountain again, 10 miles below where Manitou is. But it was just Soda Springs then, about 1½ miles above where old Colorado City is. So we moved into an emty House that didn't seem to belong to anyone.

Then more troubles come my way. Brother wanted to go to Mo. on a visit and His wife didn't, so she & I stayed and Bached there while He taken His trip. He was gone about 2 months. So there was a school going on about 2 miles from where we lived, and I went to it for a couple of months. The Teacher was a young lady, and I got along all right. She would go Home with me some times, and I would have to lead Her across the Fountain on a foot log. Right there on the foot log No. 7 was played against the queen & won with Both hands down. When we would get out about the middle of the log, right then she had to make some awful promises, only to be broken just as soon as she got me back in that school House.

On sundays I would go with a crowd of Boys and Girls on horse back to Soda Springs, (Manitou) and we would Eat our lunch and have a good time. There wasnt a house or anything there, only the spring, which was in 8 or 10 feet of the Bank of the Fountain. As we went through old Colorado City, we would stop and buy us a can of sugar which had a small little bottle of extract of lemon. We would dip up a cup of the water from the spring, put a

little sugar & a few drops of the extract in it, and then we had as fine a drink of soda pop as any one could wish for.

Well after Brother came back and school was out, He taken His wife to Denver and left Her there again to board with the Slone Family again, and Brother & I started to Texas to buy cattle. We had the Hack & mules, and there was another fellow going to Texas too, to buy cattle. He had a wagon, two men, and a pair of horses, so we all traveled along togather and had a good time.

We went by Trinidad, Red River Station, (I think now called Rattoon) Las Vegas, old Fort Sumner,[4] and to the Hondo, (where Roswell is now). There was one little shack there. It was a store, belonged to Reck & Tom Stockton. They also owned a store & Kept the stage stand at Red River Station and also had lots of cattle. They drove quite a lot of cattle every year from Texas and wintered them there, then sold them. We Expected to find a lot of Cattle at Hondo for sale, but there wasn't any. Brother & I turned back from there, and the other outfit came on to Texas, bought cattle and drove back to Colorado the next year.

We went back up to Colorado City, and my Brother had bought up about 10 or 12 head of good saddle horses. Among them was a mare that He gave $200.00 for, so He got His wife and He Hired a young fellow, and we all moved down on the Arkansas River 40 miles south of Pueblo City, on the East side of the River, and builed a Cabin or two and started to fix up for Ranching.

We always Kept one horse staked of nights to get the horses on next morning. So Brother went out One Morning and got the horse that was staked and started to look after the horses. After He had been gon about two hours, He rode up close to the Bank, on the opposite side of the River, and hollowed over to us and said that our horses had all been stolen, that He found where they had crossed the River, going south, and that there were two old rode down mexican ponys left where our horses was the night

[4] Fort Sumner was on the Pecos River in east central New Mexico.

41

before and to Keep them, and that He was agoing to follow them to Hell, if He didn't catch them this side.

So we never seen or heard of Him for at least a month.
We had about began to believe He hadn't caught them
"this side," when He Come Home, with all the horses.
But Oh, my! they were poor. He had followed them all
over New Mexico. Two mexicans had stolen them and
had sold & traded them all off for a little of nothing almost. They were professional horse thieves, but that
Ended their wild Career, as the Officers Killed them Both
in trying to arrest them.

But on Brothers way Home, He bought 600 head of
Texas yearlings from Tom Stockton at Red River Station,
which is now called Rat Toon, I think. It is just over the
Colorado line in N.M. This stream that is called Red River
makes the Little Canadian. My Brother returned to Red
River Station in Jan. some time. He returned with the
herd after having a cold drive of it. I know that there was
a lot of snow on the ground when He got to the Ranch,
and that the Boys had to scrape the snow away so as to
make their beds down.

The Cattle being to poor and wooly at that time of the
year to brand with an iron, we just run them through a
chute and Bobbed the brush of their tails off, and put red
paint on their horns. So the next summer after the cattle
shed off and got fat, we branded them with a big C on the
left side.

That fall my Brother brought 400 Cows from Mr.
Charles Goodnight, that was handling cattle for John

Chisholm.[5] We went after those Cows up to Mr. Goodnights ranch, which was at that time 15 miles up the Arkansas River from Pueblo. The next spring Brother sold all the Cattle, and we had to deliver them over North on the South Platt River about 60 miles East of Denver. This was a hard trip on "us Boys." You see I began to count myself right up among the best of them.

We only had 2 horses apiece to gather and drive those cattle on. Besides we was carrying 400 head of Cattle more than our own, to deliver for a man by the name of Hardesty, so we started out with 1400 head of Cattle. Cant say just how far it was but it was over 200 miles.

Well our old horses was poor, and we had to favor them all we could so as to get there atal. Our Cattle was all very gentle, if they were Texas Cattle, so we herded those Cattle afoot at nights so as to have our horses for day work. Working hard all day and walking around the herd about 3 hours Every night was something awful and "then some." I was young and not so tough as some of the older men was, and believe me, if I had had a goat to of been got, it certainly would of been got on that trip. But I was too young to have a goat, so for that reason only, is the whole cause why I didn't lose my goat.

When I stopped walking I would squat down to rest

[5] In 1867, Charles Goodnight "contracted to receive [John] Chisum's drives at Bosque Grande [south of Fort Sumner, New Mexico, on the Rio Grande River] on a fifty-fifty basis, allowing him a dollar a head for his risks on the trail from Texas." (J. Evetts Haley, *Charles Goodnight: Cowman and Plainsman* [University of Oklahoma Press, Norman, 1949], p. 204.)

and then I would drop off to sleep. We had 3 gards on, 2 at a time. Brother & I was on the middle gard, which is the hardest on men for two reasons. One is, that it brakes up your sleep, and the other is, after the cattle has slept and rested for an hour or so, they want to graze. One

night I was so tired & sleepy, Oh, My! and I squated down to rest a few minutes and fell asleep. So my Brother came along and caught me by the Coat Collar and gave me a pull, told me to wake up. I jumped up to my feet and said I was not asleep, but He knew better alright.

So in another half an hour or so, He found me taking another One of my little *siestas*. Well He didn't pull me up that time, call me, or hurt me, but what He did to me was a "great plenty." I sure was some mad, but He had bussiness on the far side of the herd right *now*.

We had a 40 mile drive to make on the last End of the trip without any water, but when we landed on the South Platt and delivered the Cattle the next day, we all lazed around & rested and slept all we wanted to. So then we pulled for Denver, stayed there a Couple of days and had what we called a "bully time," but now it would be called a "Hell of a time." I met one old Boy in San Antonio, Texas, about 4 years ago by the name of Mose Hays that was on that trip. It had been over 40 years since I had seen Him. We had a big laugh over my Brother waking me up on night watch.

Well we then went down into Kansas, to Abilene and to Newton. That was the summer when the "Notorious Wild Bill"[6] was city marshal of Abilene. There was a big drive there that year from Tex. and lots of cow Boys and "cow girls" too, ie., I guess you might call them that, for lots of them looked like old cows to me! They lived in a part of town called McCoys Addition. Believe me there was Certainly lots of them. That was the town where old men got young & young men got old. Abilene wasn't just only the Tom Cat's whiskers, but it was Everything Else that the Sun of a gun had or Ever will have. There never will be any more Towns & Times like those was. While Dodge City was as tough as ever a Texas herd went to,

---

[6] James Butler ("Wild Bill") Hickock (1837–76) was marshal of Abilene, Kansas, in 1871.

But it didn't have the life that Abilene had, and Abilene was tough Enough too for the majority of tenderfeet.

We bought up a herd at Newton and drove back up the Trail. We struck the Arkansas River near Ft. Dodge and drove up the River and went into winter Camps 100 miles up the River from Ft. Dodge at an old deserted Place called Ft. Auberry. We had a fine drive up the River, as we had the wide, wide world before us, behind us, and on Both sides.

There was thousands of Buffalo. The first camp we made above Ft. Dodge was about 6 or 8 miles. We Camped for dinner. That day I Killed my first Buffalo. I saw a big old Bull coming to water. He was coming into the River about 300 or 400 yards above where our wagon had camped. The River was very low at that time of the year, being in Oct., and it was wide, with channels running through the sand bars. The banks was not over 3 or 4 feet high, so I run on up the River and kept a watch out to see just where He was agoing to strack the River at. So I hid behind the Bank, and He hopped off in the water about 30 steps above me and commenced to drink. I had an old Bras jawed, rimfire winchester. I landed right behind his shoulder. He sure did come out of that River, ran about 40 yards and tumbled over. That was the fall that the Big Buffalo Hunt began, 1871.[7]

[7] The Big Buffalo Hunt, not a formally organized hunt, began with the growing market for buffalo hides and the announcement of the government policy encouraging the extermination of the buffalo so as to hasten the civilizing of the Indians. Millions of buffalo were killed within a few years after 1870.

After we had been in Camp quite a few days, there Came a bad snow storm. It was on the night of the 16th of Nov. It certainly was a bad one. That storm drove thousands of Buffalo off the Plains down on the River. We used to go out of mornings and run the Buffalo off the River Bottom to keep them from Eating up all the grass from our cattle and horses.

Two days before the storm, a man walked into our Camp carrying a winchester carbine & nothing else. He said that he had a herd of Cattle back down the River 75 miles or farther, and His horses was all played out and that he wanted to get over to the R-R- and wire His Partner that was in Montana. It was about 80 miles to the K-P-R-R-[8] North and East from the River where we was camped. He was a big fellow about 30 years old. His shoes was nearly wore out and His clothes was none too good, but we had no shoes that was large Enough for Him. If we had of happened to of had a pair, we would of given them to Him.

So the next morning was nice and warm, just a beautiful day. Brother told me to saddle up two mules that we had and to take Him just as far as I could so as to get back before night. I did and he headed for the R-R-. It was a big smooth prairie, not a Hill, Bush, or anything

[8] The Kansas and Pacific Railroad (now the Union Pacific) had crossed northern Kansas by 1871, the year in which Carpenter suggests that these events occurred. The Santa Fe, building westward, did not reach Dodge City until the summer of 1872. (*Hammond's World Atlas* [Classics Edition], [C. S. Hammond & Co., Inc., New York, 1956], plate N-14; Stanley Vestal [Walter S. Campbell], *Queen of the Cowtowns: Dodge City* [Harper & Brothers, New York, 1952], p. 2.)

Else, only Buffalo scattered over it. I went on back to Camp, got there some time late in the Evening.

Well that night the Blizzard come, and it sure was cold & bad. It snowed for about 2 days & Nights, and was cold as it Ever got to be in that Part of the world. We didn't hear anything more from Him for quite awhile, but we did finally hear that He was picked up by some one on the R-R- and His arms & legs had to be taken off. So that was the last we Ever heard of Him or His Cattle. We never Knew whether His story was true or not, but we allways had a doubt about it, but still if the fellow had a been a bad man, He could of taken my mules, and Either killed me or sent me back on foot.

Just to show you how bad this storm was I will tell you of some more poor Devils that froze to death during that storm, (only sixteen of them) and that was all there was of them. If there had been anymore, I suppose that they would of froze to death too. There was a man by the name of John Muffer, a freighter, I knew Him well. He used to freight all over Southern Colorado, had a train of about 10 or 12 teams, 8 or 10 yoke of oxon to the team, and 2 wagons to the team. He was hauling cord wood to Ft. Hays from over North of the R-R-. Got the wood off of the Smoky River or Republican River or somewhere over in that Part of the country.

He camped that night of the storm near the R-R-. I suppose that His wood was green cottonwood. Well He had quite a Bunch of steers, and when the storm Blew up He sent 2 or 3 fellows out to herd the cattle so that they

48

would not drift off, while the other fellows was getting supper etc. Soon the storm grew worse and those 2 or 3 fellows could not hold the Cattle. They were old gentle work oxen, and when the snow and wind hit them on their hind End, they would just walk right over a fellow. So one man come back to camp and told the Boss that they couldn't hold the oxen, so He sent 3 or 4 more. Soon another man come back and told the Boss that they couldn't hold them. So He said, We will all go, Knowing that if the cattle was let away that they would drift clear to the Arkansas River a distance of 75 or 80 miles.

They soon saw that all of them could not hold the cattle, and that they would freeze to death if they Kept on trying to. So He Called His men all off and went back

to the Camp. By that time the wind & snow had put their fire out, and the men was all so cold and the wind was strong and the snow was coming fast & hard so they could never get another fire started. The Boss saw that they would all freeze to death if they stayed there, and He told them that they would try to walk down the R-R- to a station called Buffalo about 12 or 13 miles.

Snuffer (the Boss) was a Big robust fellow weighing about 190 or 200 lbs. He was the only one of the 16 that got to the station, and He only lived a day or two. The others dropped along the Road and died.

One reason I remember the date so well, is because that was my Birthday. I was sweet sixteen but I "had been Kissed."

After making this camp for the winter, Brother taken the wagon & mules and went up the River to Los Animos, a town about 100 miles distance, after supplies. Had just gotten back a couple of days before this storm, and He had brought back with Him a "Kentucky Col." which was pretty bad off with lung trouble. During the time that we had been in camp, we had fixed up an old dug out that was there by putting a lot of roof poles on Top of it and a lot of buffalo hides on top of them, hung up a piece of tarp for a door, had a kinder of a fire place in the old dugout. It was sure cold and the wind blew the snow in pretty bad. The Boys taken turns holding a blanket between this man of the "Blue grass Region" and the door. After the storm had ceased, there was about 5 or 6 inches of snow on the ground, and it was as cold as it

Ever got to be in that part of the world. The wind coming back from the south, with all that snow on the ground, was just something awful and "then some."

About 2 days after the storm had ceased, we was all setting around a green cotton wood and Buffalo chip fire, when who should push the Blanket back from the door and stick his "red Irish mug" in but my Irish Sister's Brother, and calling Brother by name, saying that "His wife was out there." Right then my temptiture made only One drop, and it went below zero the first fall.

They had come in a covered Hack that they had russelled some place up about Pueblo and had got caught in the storm at a Ranch up the River and had waited until the storm was over. Brother had left Her in Denver when we started to Kan. their "Hony mooning" being over, which will come along always if you will just have a little patience. Guess that He had not Kept Her very well informed of His whereabouts and intentions, so getting anxious about the head of the Family, she started out to see what had become of Him.

Here my troubles set in again (more school days). So the four of us, Brother & Fran, Her Brother & myself, all went back up to our Ranch on the Arkansas River about 12 miles, got a place for me to board and started me in to another log cabin College. It wasn't so bad, for I had been to that College before and Knew all the Boys and girls, and liked them all, ie., I liked all the *girls*, of *course*.

The next spring we went back to camp to gather the

cattle and move them up to the Ranch. The cattle was scattered from Hell to Utah. There had been several other herds turned loose up the River above our camp to winter the same as ours was, our camp being the lowest one on the North side of the River. Our men kept all Cattle throwed back up the River, or at least tried to. Anyway we didn't have to work down below our camp very far when we went to gathering in the spring. We had to work for 60 or 70 miles up the River, but we was working towards Home.

There was one general mix up among all those through herds[9] that spring. We had lots of work. There was several different outfits and we all worked togather, had lots of big round ups and about the first of July, we all stopped rounding up and pulled out for where Ever we was going.

We got to the Ranch and turned loose, so there wasn't anything going on, any more than the general routine of ranch work, just as attending the round up, branding calves, line riding[10] etc. So I had a few more school days during the winters, which they were almost certain to come every 12 months.

I always had to work as outside man[11] during the round up. I will speak of one little incident that taken place during one of those spring round ups. Working on

[9] Herds to be delivered to distant points.

[10] Patrolling the unfenced range boundary on horseback to keep cattle turned back on their respective ranges.

[11] The "outside man" separates his employer's cattle from the roundup and drives them back to their own range. Since he represents his boss on outlying ranges, he has a position of great responsibility.

those spring round ups, early in the spring, wasn't just a little bit like going to see your Girl on sundays. You see I had a sweetheart by this time and was able to realize the difference between working in the round ups and loving my Girl on sundays. But the round ups had to be tended to, and the Girl could wait, (but sometimes they didn't).

There was a fellow by the name of Tom Russell in charge of the round up. I was along with the round up. The weather was cold and windy, for it was pretty early in the spring. The round up was awful dusty every day, for there was 2,000 Cattle or more milling around on dry & dusty ground and 7 or 8 men among them cutting out[12] and the wind blowing like the very old Devil. You can just imagine how we all looked and felt after the "shouting was over."

We had to night herd too. I had a good mount of horses, 8 or 9 head, and as good as ever was turned after a cow, and I always rode them to the full limit day or night, for I never wanted anybody to outclass me when it came to working with Cattle. I was a good roper & rider, good on brands, and allways tried to be in the right place and at the right time when Ever the "S. O. S." was "floating out." So under all my good qualities & abilities that I have just been boasting about, it was quite natural that all my Brother cow punchers would like me. Which they really did.

[12] Riding into a herd of cattle, choosing the animal to be separated from the herd, and keeping it on the move toward the "cut," or separate herd, in which it belongs.

But there was quite a few fellows living around that didn't like my Brother, because He had Caught some of them stealing His cattle and He give them Hell about it to their face but didn't try to prosecute any of them, so they wanted to do something mean against Him. And so they thought that they would frame up on me. They stood in with this round up Boss, (Tom Russell) being that Russell was about the same Kind of a "Cat" and ribbed up a fellow that worked for Russell to give me a beating, provided I didn't care to take a good cussing before the whole crowd.

This was the day before the round up was to break up. We had just turned a round up[13] loose after cutting out every thing that we wanted to, and there was a bunch of fellows setting on their horses, I guess 12 or 15 of them all ready for the show and looking as pleased as if they all held complimentary tickets. I came riding up and stopped my horse right beside my "was to be water lou." But before I tell you farther about "the bout," I want to tell you what Kind of a yellow dog I was being pitted against.

His name was Bill Nobles, and He had come up the Trail from Tex. the spring before. He was about 27 years old, weighed about 180 lbs. and was not any taller than myself. He had had a shooting scrape or two and was considdered tough, if that means anything to you. He had a big six gun hung around Him. I was 18 years old and

---

[13] Part of the job of the outside man is to attend all the roundups on ranges where he may find cattle strayed from his own range.

weighed perhaps 155 or 160 lbs. Now I expect that anyone that is reading this little unpleasentness of mine, that when they get this far along, that they will be expecting to hear of me giving that fellow an awful whipping. But if that is what they are expecting to hear, I am going to fool them. So now here I go for the "racket."

When I rode up by the side of Him, He cussed me and called me an ugly name. My horse Kinder stepped up a little, and He put His hand on His gun and said that He would burst me open. Knowing that I had been doing right by everybody and working hard, it got my goat, for I couldn't think what I had done. I asked Him and he said that I hadn't done my part on the work, so I turned to the Boss and asked Him if there had been a man on the round up that worked harder than I did. Of course He couldn't say that I hadn't but said, We had lots of cattle, and ought to of had another man along.

About that time "my man" was on the ground, and He said that He could just whip Hell out of me and that He was a better man than I was.

I said, Well thats no news to me, I think so too, Bill.

He was very quick to accept my "back down," as He thought that was what I ment. So he said right quick that settled it and started to get on His horse.

I said, Hold on Bill, all that I have just said doesn't mean that I wont fight you. So of course He had to stop.

Well I was aiming all the time to fight Him, but I haited like the Devil to do it, for I Knew that He had said it all, when He said that He was the best man, for

He was a strong made cuss. That was "when a fellow needed a friend," as the Boy in the cartoon says. I had sized up the situation and saw if I had any friends, that they were too "yellow" to even "fade." So I felt pretty lonesome but not one bit scared.

I said, Bill I am going to be nice to you and give you the best I got, and that caused a laugh.

So we laid off all unnecessaries and at it we went. He was a better boxer than I was, and His blows had more poure than mine, and it Keep me pretty well intertained Keeping off his licks. I got in a few pretty good glancing licks on his head, while He was just Knocking Hell out of me by hitting me in my side. Finally he caught me a hell of a blow on the right side of my head with His left and knocked me flat.

Now right here was where He showed the yellow dog that was in Him, instead of "the Irish" (do you get me?) for He jumped on me while I was "down, but not for the count."

I parked both of my hind feet in the pit of His Belly, Knocking Him off of me and Knocked both wind and play out of Him.

I come up from there with all the speed I had in me, and as I did, I got a good hold on His "fore top," which was pretty long. I sure did give Him a damn good wooling as long as my holt lasted, but He got me loose, and we struck a few more licks and He said, Now if you think you have got enough I'll let up.

I said right back to him, Yes I have got more than I want—and I'll give you some more of the pie.

I had got His goat when I landed in His Belly with Both of my "hind feet," see, and I knew it and so did His "Pals." So one of them steped in between us and said there was no use of all this and to stop. That suited me fine, for I was give out, but no one Knew it but myself, and He didn't insist on helping to Entertain the Boys any longer.

He called me by name and said, I think more of you now than I ever did.

And I said back to Him, Well if I think anything of you atal, its a damn sight more than I ever did.

When we got back into our wardrobes and we all rode

off, the Boss said to me, calling me by name, that I was fighting a mighty good man. I said, Tom I think you have missed it a mile by the watch, for He is not good, and He is not a man (just a plain dog).

I never saw Him again after the next day. I have all-ways wanted to see that Bird again after I growed up to be a little more seasoned than I was at that time. Well anyway I saved my credit, but I felt pretty sure that I could not whip him, for I knew that He told it straight when He said that He was the best man.

Topped Off for Texas

As THE SUMMER was passing along, we rode the range and looked after the cattle, etc., so long about the 1st of Oct. a fellow by the name of Billie Couch, that had been working for Brother nearly 2 years, took a notion that He wanted to go to town (Pueblo) and beged me to go with Him. I didnt have any money; you see I was just being raised, and they say that a fellow never pays for His raising. But I say that a fellow never gets paid for being raised, and that was the reason I had no money. I told my Brother that I wanted to go to town with Billie and wanted some money, so He gave me $15.00.

It was 40 miles to town, so it taken a day to go & a day to come, and we stayed in town 2 days. We had a pretty good time, but I couldn't Keep up my part of the Expense and that made me feel Kinder small. But Billie was a good sport, and He thought lots of me and also realized about my financial condition.

I did buy a few little things that I wanted, so we went back to the Ranch, and I got up one morning about 4 or 5 days after getting back from town and put on some of my best clothes, the Kind that would do me the best for what I had in my head. I had a good horse & saddle of my own, and rode off, as I had done lots of times before.

There had been a herd of cattle passed the ranch about 2 weeks before this, going to Kansas, so me Knowing the country clear down to the Kansas line, I figured bout where they would be by this time. I rode off from the Ranch that morning and struck out from the River, leaving the River & road about 10 miles to my right. I was heading south. There was no danger of me running into any one that far back from the Road and River, and the Ranches was pretty scattern along the River too. I rode about 50 miles before I dropped in on the River. I had slipped a little lunch in my pocket that morning while nosing around the House, but grub wasn't what I craved.

That night I staked my horse to a bush and ate my little dry lunch. There was plenty of water in holes along my route, for there had been a rain about 7 or 8 days before. I had a good saddle Blanket that suited the occasion, for I had been thinking about doing something like this every since that herd had passed down the river. So I curled up on my saddle blanket at the Bush where my horse was tied.

Well I didnt need any larm clock to call me. I felt
pretty safe that I would not see any body that Knew me
down the River, for I aimed to Keep away from the Ones
that would Know me. So I dropped in on the River the
second morning after leaving the Ranch. About 10
o'clock, struck some campers that was traveling and got
something to Eat. Then I high-tailed it on down the road.
I caught up with that herd about 150 miles farther on
down the River. My idea was to fall in with the herd,
and if I couldn't get a job, to drift along with it until I
got down the Country far Enough so I could make a town
or some settlement each day, and drift on down to Texas.
That was where I was headed for.

I had been with lots of Texas Boys, and they had told

me lots about Texas, and I liked lots of the Boys that I had met, so I was wanting to go awfully bad. I Knew that Brother wasn't going, not any ways soon, if He ever did, and that He wouldn't let me go if He could Keep me from it. So that was the reason I made the "sneak," see. Anyway it is Kinder natural for a Boy to want to do those things. But getting away from Brother was Kinder like trying to get away from my shadow, for He was Hell on a trail, (regular Indian) and I figured it that way before I left.

There was a little thunder storm that day I left, some 8 or 10 miles back out from the Ranch, and when I didn't show up that night, they began to wonder where I was at. Then the next day when I didnt come Home, they began to look for me and inquire of everybody that they saw. They first was afraid that I had been Killed by lightning, but when nothing could be found of me or my horse, they remembered about seeing me changing my clothes for better ones. So Brother He made a big guess and hit the "Bulls Eye." He figured it just as I had, and He got on one of His best bottomed horses[1] and turned His head towards that Kansas herd and throwed him in high.

I stayed all night at a Ranch that belonged to Mr. Holley and sold an old six gun to a fellow for $15.00 and that was my "financial rating." I knew Mr. Holly and had worked with Him on the round up down there a year or two before. He seemed to be anxious to Know where

[1] A horse with endurance.

I was going. I told Him that I was going to overtake that herd and that I wanted to go to Kansas for a month or two. He asked me if I didn't want to stop and work for Him a while, and that He had lots of fat horses and that some of His Boys was a little afraid to ride them. I kinder thought it was a hold up and He was playing for time to find out how come me to be making a hike like that. You see He Knew my Brother well, and He couldn't quite understand why my Brother would let me go off like that. So I said, No I didn't want to work for any one, that I wanted to go down in Kansas where I knew some good friends and visit for a month and go back to the Ranch.

This Ranch of Mr. Hollys was right at the Kansas & Colorado line. He kinder looked like He thought I was telling Him a lie, so I said good bye and went on after the herd.

I caught up with it at noon that day. They were all Eating dinner when I rode up. The outfit all Knew me, for I had stayed pretty close to them for a day or two while passing through our range. They said, Get down and unsaddle and have dinner, so I did. Wanted to Know what I was doing riding around so far from Home. I said that I wasnt riding near as far from Home as I will be in another week or two.

The outfit got ready and started out for their Evening drive. I walked out to where my horse was grazing and led Him up and was putting my saddle on him when I looked back up the road and saw my Brother about 200 yards off coming as straight on my trail as an Indian ever went to water. Well sir that was one time when this fellow didn't need a friend. At least I didn't want one trailing up. I believe at that moment, if I had a Known He was agoing to shoot me dead, I wouldn't have been unhappier than I was right then. I wasn't afraid of Him trying to make me go back or balling me out or anything like that, but I Knew He never would go back without me. I Knew that I was going back with Him too, but still I didn't want to.

So I walked out and met Him, and He began to cry and I did too. Then He talked very affictionate to me and said many things to me about "the past" which was "very touching," and beged me to return with Him. So all that got my goat, and what Else could I do but go back with Him?

That fall he branded me 100 head of nice heifer calves, but I didn't want them. Would much rather of had a R-R- ticket for Texas. But He promised me that we would go as soon as He could see out and get His business all straightened up.

So that winter I had more school days, and they were the last too. Quit my log cabin college just three days before school was out, not on any other account, "only my health."

Our Teacher was a man about 26 years old by the Name of Billie Musgraves. Just 3 days befor school was out, during the Noon hour, most of the Boys was playing ball, and the girls had went down on a little creek which was about a quarter of a mile off to get some tooth brushes, ie., that was what they said they were going to do and none of us Boys doubted their word, for it would be a mighty mean Boy that would doubt a girls word. So my sweethearts brother & I parked our carcasses out on the sunny side of the house. (You Know I have allready told you that I had a sweetheart, which I guess most all Boys have until they learn better.) So the Teacher come out where we were and saw us having a nice quite little game of seven up.

I had the deck in my hand, just about ready to turn Jack from the bottom, when He said to me, Let me see those cards. So I handed the cards to Him, and He turned and walked into the House.

This Boy was about 19 years old and as strong as a young Bull. His first name was Leon (have forgotten his last name) so we got up and shook ourselves, kinder like a horse after wallowing, and followed Him into the House.

Leon said to Him, Mr. Musgraves those are my cards, and I want them.

He said, I'll look after those cards, and I am not agoing to give them to you. (There had been 2 or 3 other big Boys that had trailed in to see what was agoing to happen.) (Well they hadn't long to wait.)

So Leon told Him that He would much rather He would steal them than to take them that way.

Then the Teacher rushed at Him, and it looked as though He was trying to get Leon by the throat. They shoved each other over Benches, stove, and Everything

Else that happened to be in their way. The Teacher was a strong fellow but taller by a couple of inches than Leon. There was a Bench against the wall just under the Black Board, so He pushed Leon back against the Bench, and Leon stepped up on the Bench and with His Back against the wall, had pretty solid backing. Some time during the shoving act, the Teacher had got His thumb in Leon's mouth, and Leon had taken a case of the lock-jaw. So when Leon got on top of that Bench, He sure did give Him one awful hard Kick. Being up higher than the Teacher, He hit rather low, and should have been called a foul according to the queen Berry rules of fighting.

There was a Big old Boy by the name of Felix Kellog looking on like He was refereeing the bout. Leon must have felt a little "yellow streak" coming up His back, for He called out and said, Help me Felix, but never opened His mouth, for He still had the Teachers thumb.

So Felix said, Just hold your holt Leon. You have got him whipped.

By that time the Teacher was getting pretty sick from that Kick and Leon grazing on His best thumb, His right. So Felix said, Mr. Musgraves when you get enough I'll make Leon quit.

He said, I have enough of this.

Then Felix said, Turn him loose Leon, and He did.

So we got our Books and quit College, me being two games on Leon & Leon being a "Hoss" on the Teacher.

I went Home with Leon which was about 1½ miles.

67

We hadn't been Home very long until Leon's two Sisters came, saying that school had been turned out rather Early. Next day those old farmer Trustees, (you see it was a farming Neighbor-hood) was setting around that old log cabin school house like Buzzards around a dead horse, and that day turned out to be the last day of school. So that completed my education in Books, but not otherwise, for I have learned several things since.

Well the rest of that spring & summer there wasn't anything going on only the general routine of cow work, the same as there was in all other open ranges where there was lots of cattle. Being pretty dry that year, Brother thought it best to gather the cattle and move them over East about 75 miles near the K-P-R-R- where Range was good and there wasnt any Ranches or Cattle nearer than 40 or 50 miles.

So we did. We struck camp about 10 miles from a little town called Kit Carson, on the R-R-. It was named I supposed after Kit Carson, the old Indian trader. We stopped on a dry creek called Big Sandy, about 12 miles from where Gen. Shivington Killed about 400 Navaho Indians in the spring of 1864 and got Kicked out of the Army for doing the right thing.[2] The water stood in

[2] On November 27, 1864, Colonel J. M. Chivington led a force of 900 soldiers in a surprise attack on a group of Chief Black Kettle's Cheyennes, near Fort Lyon in southeastern Colorado, south of Kit Carson. In this reprisal for Indian attacks on stage and freight lines east of Denver, the troops killed mostly old men, women, and children. The Indian Department called the battle a massacre, and the Colonel's conduct was investigated by a committee of Congress, which condemned the action as "disgracing the uniform of United States soldiers and officers." However, the Colorado

Holes along on this Creek, some of them being 2 or 3 miles apart and some farther than that. The west, or south Side of this Creek, was sand Hills, which was about 35 or 40 miles through them. There was a creek called Rush creek back in those sand Hills about 12 miles from Camp. On the North or rather the East side of this creek, was a smooth prairie as far as your Eyes could see, not hill or bush or anything else, only just a wide, wide world covered with short buffalo grass which was very fine.

We had about 1500 head of Cattle of our own, and there was perhaps 150 head of big steers among them that we aimed to ship to the Kansas City market. There was an old Bachelor that lived on the River below our Ranch about 12 miles, and He had gathered about 25 head of steers of His and threw in our herd and went along Himself. He aimed to ship His when we shipped ours, which we was aiming to do in a day or two after getting to where we was going to stop. We got in on the creek where we aimed to stay, in the middle of the day, watered the cattle well and left them. So that Evening late some of us rode out around the cattle and gentlely turned all the outside back a little and left them for the night.

Next morning was a nice sunny morning, and

Brother told me to ride out and turn all the outside cattle back towards the water while the rest of them started to work to make a dugout. I saddled up, hung my winchester on my saddle and rode off around the cattle, turned all of them back, as I supposed. But I guess I must have rode over the trail where a Bunch of big steers had passed out and I didn't see it, not thinking that they would just get up and high tail it back for the ranch. So I was careless about it, and too, I was trying to get an antelope to take back to camp.

That evening Brother rode out to help turn the cattle in, and He missed a lot of those big steers. He made a welter round out on the outside and saw where they had trailed out the night before. He had us to throw the herd on bed ground[3] and said to herd them night & day until we got those steers cut out to ship and that He would try to overtake those that had left, and also gave me a pretty good Balling out about being so careless as not to see that Trail. So He hiked out after them. They were easy trailed, for it was very sandy where they had to pass along.

Well there was several head of this old Bachelors steers missing, so He felt sore at me about it. The next morning some of us was eating breakfast and one or two holding the herd. This old Guy and I was soping molasses out of the same plate, and He began to quarrel at me about losing the cattle. I felt bad enough at myself without Him Belly acheing at me, and besides Bro. had hurt

[3] The place where cattle are halted to spend the night.

my feelings about it. So I give it right back to Him just a little bit stronger than He gave it to me.

So He jumped up and Kicked our plate about 20 feet, called me by name, and said that He could trim my lamp.

I got up and looked at Him for about a minute, and said, Well if you think they need trimming, why in the Hell dont you do it.

So he come up to me like a regular John L—[4] with His arms up in front of His face. I let fly my right fist and caught him in the side of the neck, a glancing blow, but it Knocked Him partly down, and He caught on one hand to keep from gowing down flat.

I waited for Him to get up and then I moved up towards Him, and He said, Now you stop that, you g—— d—— fool. So I turned around and went to the herd.

After a little while He came riding to where I was and was in a better humor than He had been on this whole trip. Afterwards some of the Boys asked me why I didn't give it to Him good, but I said that I didn't want to. So it was all over, but I don't think it was all forgotten, (by Him anyway).

Well Brother got back that night with about 40 head of steers which He had overtaken, and said that He saw where about 20 head had went on back towards Home. The next day we cut all the steers out and carried them to Kit Carson and shipped them to K-C-.[5] Brother and my

---

[4] John L. Sullivan (1858–1918), American heavyweight champion prizefighter, 1887–92.

[5] Kansas City.

"friend" the old Bachelor went with the cattle, and the other Boys and myself kinder loose herded[6] the rest of the cattle until they came back from K-C-.

Then we all flew in and made a pretty good dug out. Then they all pulled back to the river, (or Home rather). This was about Nov., some time near the middle. They said that they would be back about Xmas, so I was left alone.

They had left me about 20 head of saddle Horses. I was supposed to line ride on the cattle etc. I got along pretty well, it was all new range and the grass sure was fine.

So Xmas week came, and at the End of the week Bro. and two of the Boys came back. They had the wagon and a horse or two. They found everything in pretty good shape, but the cattle was scattered down the Creek for 7 or 8 miles which was quite natural.

About the 5th of Jan. there came one of the darnest snow storms, and cold, (the suffering cats) I dont think I ever did see it so cold. There was four moon dogs at night and four sun dogs in the day time. If you never have been in a cold country, you may not Know just what I mean. They are big spots on each side of the moon or sun, but it sure has to be Cold to see those "puppys."

I never will forget the 8th of Jan. after the storm had cleared off. All 4 of us taken the wagon and went down the creek about 4 miles to a little green cotton wood grove

[6] Let the cattle scatter somewhat, yet kept them within handling distance.

and got some green fire wood to mix in with the cow chips, which was our main fuel. That day was still and clear. I'm not agoing to tell you that it was cold, will just leave that to your own imagination. I never did see as beautiful a sight before or since in the heavens. There was four sundogs and four circles, some larger than the others all linked into Each other almost straight up in the heavens. I never did see anything so pretty as that was, and I never can forget it.

Well that storm relieved us of nearly all the cattle.

There was perhaps 150 head or about that number that did not drift clear away clear out of reach entirely, only to be gathered up in the spring round ups.

After this cold spell, as soon as the weather warmed up a little, the outfit pulled back to the Ranch, leaving me alone again. Of course there wasnt much to do, only cook, eat, and look after the saddle horses. I would go to town once in a while to see if there was any letters for me, but I wasn't writing any and therefore wasn't expecting any, (not even from my sweetheart). I was thinking a lot more about good cutting & roping horses than I was about the Girls at that time.

After that storm, there was a world of antelope drifted in around near our camp. I would see a bunch coming to water and I would hide under the Bank and Kill 2 or 3 Every day and sometimes more. I would take their insides out and pile them up in front of the dugout like so many sacks of corn, and when I would get about 15 or 20 I would take them to Kit Carson and get a dollar a piece for them. I had got an old wagon and 3 or 4 old poor ponys in a trade, so I had a wagon to haul things in. It was cold all the time and the antelope would freeze solid the first night and stay froze. So that way I passed the time pretty well.

Along about the middle of Feb. a first cousin of mine, and a fellow by the name of Jeff Steel, came to my camp and stayed bout a week. They came from Pueblo, which was about 150 miles. Steel had Kill a man and was Keeping out of the way for a little while until the fog had cleared away. He had married my cousin's sister, which made Him a cousin of mine also.

When spring opened up, (being the spring of 1875) the outfit came back, and we started out on the round ups to gather our cattle back to the Ranch, (near Kit Carson). We worked all summer and got Every cow that we could find, including what we hadn't gathered the fall before, for we aimed to sell out Everything and go to Tex.

We sold all the cattle to a firm, (or company) by the name of Kankle & Lafener, and they was to receive them in the R-R- Pens at Kit Carson. So we worked all the summer getting our cattle gathered, and after we got them all in, or about all, we cut out all the yearling steers, for we had sold them to another party, and had to be delivered over on the head of the Republican River, a distance as near as I remember of about 90 miles. So brother and some of the other Boys started off with the yearlings, leaving me & another Boy to look after the cattle etc.

On the 19 of Sept. there came a cold rain and turned off to a snow storm. It lasted a day and a night, so when it cleared off, there wasn't left a cow on the range. All gone. Me & the other Boy lit out on their trail, which was easy to see, for the storm had drove them west right into the sand Hills and made sign enough for 5,000 head of cattle.

It was about noon when we got topped off,[7] so we fol-

[7] Prepared. Also "To ride first, to take the rough edges off a horse." (Ramon F. Adams, *Western Words: A Dictionary of the Range, Cow Camp, and Trail* [University of Oklahoma Press, Norman, Okla., 1946], p. 167.)

lowed until night, but we had begun to catch up with the tail end of the herd. They had gone on to Rush Creek, a distance of about 12 miles from the camp. There was

plenty of water & the grass was as fine as it could be, and the storm had let up and so had they. We found them scattered along this creek for about 4 miles.

We rode on up the creek until we thought we were

about above them all, then we struck camp for the night. It wasnt much of a strike, for all we had to do was to unsaddle, but we roped a fat calf first and then staked our horses out. So we had calf ribs "galore" but no salt. Anyway we were happy, for we knew that we had our Cattle. You see I hadn't forgotten what had happened the fall before.

There was about 3 inches of snow on the ground, but the weather was not much cold. We layed on our Backs that night and covered with the North star. Didn't need any larm clock to wake us up by next morning.

We filled up on more meat and tied some to our saddles and fell in after those old "gevelers" as soon as we could see good. We drove back down the creek, gathering them as we went, for they was not far from the creek. We got them all togather and headed them back on their back trail towards camp. We didnt take time to cook any more meat, for when we got those old cows togather, we didn't want them to get scattered on us any more. So we hit the ball and kept it arolling.

When we got within about 1½ miles of the camp late that Evening, we met Bro. with the other Boys coming on the trail. Had two horses a piece and two Extra for us and a pack horse. They had just got back from delivering the yearlings, and they Knowed what had happened and had rigged up their pack outfit and lit out on our trail. They was sure glad to see us coming trailing back with all the cattle, but as for being glad, they didn't have anything on us, for we was glad to see them too.

We never turned those cattle loose again. We delivered them in Bunches at the R-R- as "the man" wanted them. So we had them all shipped out by the latter part of Oct. or perhaps a few days Earlier.

Then we taken all our outfit and joined in with a roundup that was going on down the Ark. River. We got the most of the scattering cattle that was out, on that work, which was broke[8] near Los Animos, where Conkle & Lafever, (the man we sold to) was running a slaugher hous. So we turned over the Cattle that we had gathered on that work to them, at the slaugher house, so that wound up our Cow business. We then sold all our saddle horses to a man by the name of John Pramers, which was one of the wealthyest men in Southern Colorado, and was married to a regular old black Blanket Cheyenne Indian squaw, but never the less, He was as fine a gentleman as anyone ever met. He had several "little warriors." There was quite a number of reasons told by the people, just why He married this squaw, but really no one Knew.

We went back up the River to the Ranch, which was about 90 miles, to get ready to leave Colorado for the "Lone Star State" of Texas, where my Brother & I Expected to make our future Home. We stayed at the Ranch about two weeks, and during that time Brother & His wife settled all their little arguments which had taken place in the last 10 years by dividing the "Jack Pot." You Know the most of the Irish are Catholics, so she was no exception to the rule, & she made one out of Him too. You allso

[8] Finished. This usage seems analogous to "broke camp."

Know that they dont believe in divorces, so that is why they parted as man & wife to never meet again, after saying to each other, Bye bye, my Honey.

Well I have told you that I had a sweetheart also. Well I did, and she was a "real Tweelie," too. We thought heaps of Each other, but you Know true love dont never run smoothly over the rough rout that it generally has to travel. We had our little troubles, (nothing serious) so we had been Kinder froze up for quite a little while, and me being busy all the summer gathering Cattle, did not get to see one another very often, and when we did, just met "as acquaintances," not as sweethearts, each one wanting the other to "thaw out" first, see. But we neither one did.

About 3 or 4 days before we was to pull out for Los Animos, where we would take the train for Texas, Her Bro. Leon Came by the Ranch.

He said to me, I have a letter for you, do you want it. And the way He looked at me, ment oceons.

I said, Yes, so He gave me the letter. It was full of "Baby talk," and my temperature rose to bout 120 in the shade. So next morning I put on all my good looks and saddled up and rambled off up the River with the happy thoughts of Kissing and makeing up.

Now right here I am agoing to stop and ask a question. But I know it will never be answered. Why does a woman run from a man, where really and truly, she wants to run to Him? When I got close to Her House, which was right on the public road, I saw Her in the garden, and she saw

me too. I was not over 20 steps from Her, and she run in the House. So I just rode on up the road a couple of miles and taken dinner with some friends of mine, told them good bye, and started back Home.

Well I had to pass back by Her House, see, so when I got in sight of the House, I saw that she had parked Her Self out on the front galerry. The road was not over 15 or 20 steps from the House, so I just looked off the other way and rode on by. But it sure did hurt, ie., if I know how to tell the truth.

But I am going to get ahead of my trip to Tex. a few years and tell you what a dirty trick I done Her. I heard from Her through other Parties once in a while, and Knew that she was still single. After about 4 years in Tex. I got a letter one day telling me that my old sweetheart had got married, so then I wrote to Her for the first time after coming to Texas. I said all the sweet & loving things to Her that I could possible think of, calling Her all Kind of sweet names and told Her that I was coming after Her and would bring Her back to Texas with me. But I forgot "of course" to give Her my P.O. address so to be sure she didn't answer that letter. Wouldn't have known where to have written to if she had a wanted to.

So a few years after that, I met a Boy up in Dodge City that used to live with us that happen to be working for Her Husband on a Ranch at the time she got "that sweet letter." She showed Him the letter, and He said that she bawled around the House for a day or two just like a doggy calf, but no one but Him Self Knew why. I guess the reason I did that, was because I still loved Her and Knew that I had lost Her, so thats that.

But like all other warriors, I was to meet my water Lou later on, as you will see.

The Wide, Wide World

Now GOING BACK to where I dropped off. We got on the train at Los Animos and went down to Mo., where we had one sister living and lots of other Kin Folks. I had a pretty good time running around with my pretty cousins & nieces until I was taken down with the measles. So that put a "quietus" to my good time.

When I got so I could travel, we hit the R-R- for Texas, got off at Denison, that being the terminus of the M-K & T at that time, (Feb. 10th, 1876) the Texas Central being the only R-R- in Texas at that time, (if I am not mistaken).[1] We went out north of Denison about 10

[1] On January 15, 1877, the Galveston, Harrisburg, and San Antonio Railroad, which had begun construction in 1852, reached San Antonio, Texas. The second railroad in Texas was the Houston and Texas Central, construction of which began at Houston in 1853. On March 18, 1873, the Houston and Texas Central reached Denison, Texas, where it made a junction with the Missouri, Kansas, and Texas Railroad. (*The Works of Hubert Howe Bancroft* [The History Company, Publishers, San Francisco, 1890], Vol. XVI, pp. 570–72; V. V. Masterson, *The Katy Railroad and the Last Frontier* [University of Oklahoma Press, Norman, Okla., 1952], pp. 188–89.)

miles where a cousin of our's lived and visited with Him for about a week, and got all the pointers that He was able to give us, which was quite a few, for He had lived in Texas over 30 years.

So we went back to Denison. There was a young man by the Name of Abb Newell met us there. He had been working for us up in Colorado for a couple of years and wanted to come to Texas with us. He had come on down into Kansas and had been having a good time while we was in Mo. We bought a little pair of mules & a Hack, camp outfit etc., and started out to Explore Tex. We had some more Cousins living in Johnson Co., in what was called the Cross Timbers not over 35 or 40 miles south of Ft. Worth. We went to see them and visited there a Couple of weeks. Then we started out in Earnest.

We drifted over in Eastern Texas through our lack of not Knowing just where we ought to go, for you see Texas is a mighty big country, and if a fellow dont Know a lot about it, He is liable to go where it dont suit Him, and that is what we did. We got down as far as Hemstead, which was the terminus of the Tex. Central. Then we went back up the country a ways and turned west, and drifted on down south until we got down below Austin, I think about 25 or 30 miles.

There we met a herd of cattle headed for the west. They had stampeded a few nights before, ran over the owner and broke His arm, so He wanted to sell them and go back home to Hallettsville. Well we was not long in buying Him out, bought wagons, horses, & cattle. It wasn't a large herd, only a few over 700 head, all stock cattle[2]—3 year old steers was classed in as stock cattle in those days. We drove this herd up north of Ft. Griffin[3] and turned them loose on the open Range, on a creek called Boggy in Throckmorton Co.

There was a good many Cattle in the Country, and Cattle drifted in the winter time in that part of the country. Millet & Irwin had about 20,000 head of through cattle turned loose on the range north of us about 25 or 40 miles, so when we started out on the general round ups in the spring to gather our Cattle, which was a general mix up, we found ours the same as Everybody Else found theirs, (scattered from Hell to Breakfast). That was the time when a fellow had to sleep a-running if He aimed Ever to get His Cattle gathered. There was outfits that went as far as 100 miles South and Even farther and worked back.

Millets & Irvin worked lots of men, and some of them the damnest thieves that any man ever saw. Millets & Irvin had a big Government Contract to furnish Beef for the Indians at Ft. Sill in the Indian Ty., and they began to drive Early in the spring, and they drove Everything that got in their herd if some one wasn't right there Jonny on the spot to cut it out. Cattle was poor and the hair was long on the Cattle, and it made it hard to see brands. So they got off with many a cow and steer that belong to some one Else. The people Kicked so much

[2] Breeding cattle.
[3] Fort Griffin is in northern Shackleford County, just south of the Throckmorton County line. It is now a Texas state park.

about it that Millets & Irvin agreed to throw their Cattle
all togather and let the people get their Cattle.

Well they did. They threw all that they could get
togather into two herds, about one half of a mile apart.
They claimed that there was about 17,000 head in those
two round ups. Now just stop and think for a second, and
see if that many Cattle, with the hair long on them and
them telling the people to go ahead and cut their Cattle
out. Does that mean anything to you? Well I should say

that it didn't mean much, and still it did, for what a fellow left there in those big herds was liable, and damn liable, to go to Sill and make food for the "Poor Indians." There was where good Cow horses and good Cow Boys meant something. I'll not try to say about how many men was at that round up, but I expect that there was more than ever was at any round up before or since.

Well we worked until up into the latter part of July on the round ups, then I was sent back thru in the fall for the fall round ups. In the mean time, we had moved over southwest about 100 miles or more, on the Clair Fork[4] of the Brazos River at the mouth of Sweetwater Creek, 25 miles Northwest of where Abilene is today. I did not tell you that we bought 400 head more cattle just before we turned our herd loose on Boggy Creek, which made up 1,100 head.

After the fall work was all over, we was out I guess about 80 or 90 head, which wasn't so bad after taken Everything into consideration. I'll say right here, that by being a *cow hand* among "cow hands & cow thieves," that it saved us many a cow.

I had about 300 head of my own, and I taken quite an interest in the cow business. I would sell a Bunch of fat steers in the fall to the beef buyers and would go up into Mo. among the corn fed Girls and blow in, come back as soon or just a little sooner before I got broke. Then I was good for another 12 months hard work, sleeping on

---

[4] Clear Fork of the Brazos River, which runs north from Taylor County, through Jones and Throckmorton counties, to the Brazos.

wet saddle Blankets, working on round ups, line riding, "laying out with the dry stock,"[5] etc.

When we first settled on the Clair Fork, 25 miles was our nearest Neighbor. There was quite a few buffalo still left in the country after the Big Hunt, a world of wild horses, and other small game, such as Deer & Antelope and thousands of wild turkeys. So the years passed by pretty smooth until the spring of 1880. Then I had some more grief, for my Dear Brother taken down sick with the flux and only lived about 15 days, died on the 9th of March 1880.

I had been up in Mo. that winter for a couple of months, and had only been back a short time when He died. He willed me all His property, and it seemed right to Everybody Else that He should, for I had done all the hard outside work through rain or shine and had been the "real true blue" and He Knew it too and also appreciated it and showed His appreciation by doing what He did.

Now I will tell you again that He was a catholic and was not divorced, so right here is where my red headed Irish sister and I met again. She come down all wound up like a 8 day clock and tried to take all His property, but she soon found out that she couldn't get only a part of it. He had divided up with Her when we came to Tex. but that didn't mean anything now, so she Came in for half. Cattle was pretty cheap at that time, and she was willing to take $6,000.00 and pull Her freight.

[5] Cattle that do not give milk; usually meaning dry cows.

Then was the first time that I ever borrowed any money, and it just scared the stuffing out of me. I had to mortgage every Blooming thing that I had and to stand for a Hell of a lot of pretty hard advice to boot. Bankers can sure tell it straight to a poor Devil when they think that they have Him in a corner. I was all right, but I was scared.

Well I drove quite a nice little Bunch of Beef steers down to Ft. Worth that fall, it being the terminus of the T & P-R-R-[6] at that time. I shipped them to Chicago and went with them. Didn't only get $20.00 per head for them, ie., I mean they net me about that. So when I got back to Ft. Worth, I traded a fellow that I used to Know on the Range a half interest in my outfit and bought half interest in a big Livery stable He had there. That was the wrong thing for me to have done, but that note & mortgage was Eating on me, so after making that trade and with my steer money, I was able to get out of debt, and that made me feel good.

I run the Ranch & my partner run the stable & the women. We had the Bigest business in Ft. Worth, and at that time Ft. Worth had began to get busy, believe me. We had a $10.00 foreman, builed a Big Brick stable extra, had quite a lot of Big fine street Hacks, kept a Herse, and was just "raising Hell generally." I would come down about every two or three months and help "gather in the crop," (do you get me?)

You know that I told you quite a ways back in this

[6] The Texas and Pacific Railroad.

story I finally met my water Lou. Well I did, but I had several fierce Battles with old Cupid before I did. But finally what I thought was the impossible, turned out to be the possible. So I sold out, and we both taken a different route. I went the Chisholm trail, and he went the morphine route. This all happened in 1882.

I drove a herd of 1,800 steers to the Territory that year, turned them loose on Word & Reeds Ranch on Beaver Creek near Camp Supply,[7] went back to Ft. Worth that fall and sold those 1,800 fat steers to Word & Reed, range delivery.[8] The next spring in 1883 a fellow by the

[7] Camp Supply, now Fort Supply, is in northwestern Woodward County, Oklahoma, down the Canadian River from Beaver Creek. Probably referring to the same drive, W. M. Wilkinson, of Stanton, Texas, wrote to Carpenter on September 21, 1921:

"Dear Old friend. Receved your Letter Some time Back. Sure was Glad to heare from you and to Know that you are Still on the Turff. Bill, Seams in your Letter that you doant Remember me. I am the Kid that Went up the trail with you and Andy Waters and Joe McDial and Bud Curr [Kerr?] about 35 years ago or moore. The Last time I Saw you and your wife was at the Star Hotel at Anson, Texas. You was Runing the ◇ wagon and I was working for the *CALL*. When I went with you on the trail wee Started from Nolin Spring in Johnson County [south of Fort Worth] with tow thousand Steers Banded △ on the Left Side, took them to the Rin Ranch on Beaver Creek Eight Miles west of Ft. Camp Suply. Sim Holsteen was Runing the RIN Ranch for Old Jim Reed and Tom Ward. I stayed at the Rin Ranche until December and I Rode your Big white mare that you got from Dave Godwin. Well Bill I always glad to heare from Some of the Old Cow boys. So if you Ever happen to come to Stanton I want you to Bee Sure to Hunt me up Because I allway Glad to meet Some of the old timers. I got Buford's Picture yet tho it fadded so Bad that you wouldent Know it. So Bill I Ring off for this time Hoping to meat you Some time and then I Talk about old Jones County. Your friend, W. M. Wilkinson."

[8] An arrangement whereby the buyer pays for what the seller claims to own, then goes out on the range and rounds up his purchase himself.

name of Hudson & myself taken a contract to put up 9,000 head of Cattle to be delivered at Holly, right at the Kansas & Colorado line on the Arkansas River a little over 100 miles above Dodge City. We also bought up about 2,500 head more to take along to sell on the open market. We had another fellow interested with us in this herd of 2,500.

We drove these cattle, nearly 12,000 head, in three big herds. We went the western Trail, crossed Red River at Doans Crossing.[9] I drove the lead herd. My herd consisted of all steers, from two year olds up to four year olds. I had over 3,500 in my herd. We first started out from Bosque Co. with about 5,000 head and drove to Henrietta. There we got in two herds from Coleman Co. and 1,800 cattle shipped in from Fla., then we pulled out. We had over 4,000 in one herd.

When I left Henrietta I had with my herd 8 riding men with the cattle, myself, horse rangler & cook. But oh, my! those steers could scatter in 15 minutes so that it looked like we never would get them rounded up again. But they worked fast when we started to move them in together, and it didnt take no time hardly until we would have them all rounded up and on the bed ground.

After we crossed Red River and throwed out on the North side for to noon,[10] I found one of my men asleep on herd with His saddle under His head. That was the End

[9] Doan's Crossing, or Doan's Store, was an important crossing on the Red River, downstream from the Texas Panhandle border on the Dodge City Trail.

[10] To hold the herd during the noon period.

of his trip. All the rest of my men was good men. There was several negroes. I had taken all the meanest horses in my outfit and had all the best riders too. Those coons was all good riders & so was my white Boys.

When we got up on the Big Washitaw River, two of those coons had a falling out, and they just shot Hell out of Each other but neither one was Killed. I layed over that half of day, thinking that we would get to plant them Both, but we didn't. You see that left us pretty short handed, only six of us with that big herd, but we had them well broke in by that time and didn't see any big cause to worry. We had the wide, wide world to drift along over and nothing to bother us, plenty of grass & water, and a good negro cook.

The next morning after the fight we threw those two coons in the wagon and hit the Trail. That day at noon, as luck would have it, an old Boy came riding up to camp from back down the Trail on his way to Dodge City. I Knew Him on the range down in west Texas and Knew Him to be a good one too, so I hired Him and then we was "heeled." The negros got all right then and when we got within about 50 miles of Dodge, I put them on the stage, and sent them on.

When we got there, the Arkansas River was higher than a mad cats back, and we had to wait nearly two weeks for it to get so we Could put all those herds across. Dodge City was in full Bloom, you can take it from me. There was a big drive there that year, and believe me, you could sure get a fast run for your money. Dodge City is so well known that I will not try to tell you anything about it.

We got across the River and pulled on for Holly station. We had sold this extra herd of 2,500 to the same outfit, so my Partner & this fellow that was interested with us in the 2,500 met us at Dodge. They come up on the Train. This fellow, I will Call Him Tom for I think any fellow that pulled the stunt that he did while in Dodge, deserves a name. He was one of those fellows that had made so much money and made it so quick that He thought He was certainly It, and He "was" as it turned out. He wore a $1,000.00 watch, a $400.00 stud, and God only Knows what His rings was worth, but he had a Batch of them. He certainly did prove Hisself a "ladies Gentleman." Some of those Dodge City Guys baited Him with two gold Bricks, and He bit at it and got "hooked." And a very Dear Texas friend of His was agoing to buy one but didn't. They turned out to be copper and worth about $3.50, so that taken the play out of Him. Of course, the fellow that sold them "side stepped."

We got to our Place of delivery and helped brand the Cattle out and all rolled our dough for Tex, sold all the horses that was with my herd and taken the others back to Texas. We settled up with all the men, which was about 30. They all went back on the Train but 4 or 5 which went back with the wagon & horses. I spent the bigest part of the winter in Ft. Worth that winter, although me & my Partner, (Hudson) bought up a good many cattle along towards spring.

We put up 6,000 head and fited them out for the Trail for a man by the name of Jessie Evans. We also shipped a good many Cattle to market, (fat cattle) and we sent a herd to Dodge city also. It was not a large herd, only about 1,000 head, all young steers, ones & twos.[11] About the time the herd got to Dodge, I went up on the Train.

There was a good big drive there that year too. There was lots of buyers from the northwest, but they wasn't buying, just holding off, trying to get better prices. I bought a nice herd of 1,000 head of two year old steers and put them in our herd. I held the herd one month and when I sold, I had to take $1.00 less on the head than I gave for them. Anyway, they helped the sale of our other Cattle, for the ones I bought was dandies, and our others was not nothing extra.

This was the year that nearly all the cow men went to the wall, 1884. When I got back to Texas, I found that my Partner had been plunging to beat Hell, buying and shipping beef cattle. He had a mania for it, and I knew it, and He promised me that He wouldn't buy any more while I was gone. I found out that He had lost a lot of money, so we had about 1,400 head of stock on hand when I went away. He had moved them out west where I had turned loose the herd in 1876. I knew that country and He didn't, and I knew that it was played out and there was a drouth out there too. I Knew that those cattle was up against it, so I thought the best thing I could do was to sell out to Him and get all the security that I could.

[11] One- and two-year-olds.

So I did and taken a mortgage on the cattle, and had about 3 of His Brothers to sign a Note for $24,500.00.

The Brothers was all pretty well fixed at that time. But along towards spring He made a contrack with an Eastern man to put Him up 6,000 head of yearling steers up in Kansas and got a big lot of money advanced on the contract, and His Brothers signed that contract too. Well that winter there was an awful die up out where those 1,400 Cattle was, and damned near all my mortgaged Cattle died.

He bought up 6,000 head for His contract alright and started North with them. After He got off a little ways with the herds, He sold 2,000 head of those contracted, to another Party, and was fooling along with the others, not trying to deliver them. In fact I couldn't see what He was trying to do with them unless He was trying to sell them too. So "His man" heard about what He was doing and come back to Texas from some place up about New Jersy and attached the 4,000 head that He had on the trail. Then they had some Kind of an agreement through the court to sell the cattle to a couple of men on time, by the name of Reed & Odom.

They put the cattle up in the Pan Handle, and it was an awful hard winter. The cattle all died. Reed & Odom was busted "wide open." So the Eastern man, He sued my expartner & all three of His Brothers and got big judgments against the whole "Rush." Then He cleaned up on the whole "smear." That played Hell with my securities, cattle all dead and securities no good.

95

In the mean time I had soaked the $24,500.00 Note for $2,500.00 to an old money loaner (or *thief*, as it turned out). If He had a collected the interest on the Note, which I proved He could have done, it would of paid off the loan; but He didn't do it.

You see my expartner had a loan with Him too, and this old thief held a mortgage on a big lot of stuff and allowed Him to sell it and would not collect my interest when it was past due, but left Him keep the money. So when my Loan came due, He sold them Notes and bought them in. I was broke and had no way of getting the money to pay off the loan so as to get that Note back. It wouldn't been worth a damn at that time if I had a got it back.

I just let it go for a year or more, then I thought that I would sue this old Devil for not collecting the interest & principal, which was all due at the time He let my expartner, (the maker of the Note) sell all that mortgaged stuff, and after, pay this thief what was coming to Him. So I went to a law firm and told them that I would give them a third of all they could get out of it. They wrote around to His lawyers, (I mean the thief's) and of course they discouraged my lawyers and they wouldn't take the case. Then another fellow (a Negro) holding a mortgage on cattle, sued my expartner & this old Devil togather, for $2,500.00, and I got another law firm to intervene in the suit for me. Well there was another fellow intervened in the suit too. Me and the Negro got a judgement. They gave the Negro some cattle that He had sold this expartner of mine, and some way this old thief became responsible for the debt. They proved that all the cattle died at the same time the 1,400 did, and they gave me a judgement of $3,264.00.

This old thief's lawyers got all the judgements set aside on the grounds that the verdict they gave the Negro was not an inteligent verdict because the cattle was all dead, and they should have given Him the value of the Cattle. You see He held a mortgage on the cattle for $2,000.00.

We all had a new trial in about 6 months, and they put one of those lawyers on the stand that I had tried to get to take my case two years before I intervened. So He testified to it. We went through with the whole business just as we did at the other trial, only this old thief proved His character & plead limitation all at the same time. When the Judge read His charge, He charged the jury to find against me on the grounds of limitation, (in other words, I was legally high jacked) so that was that. Limitations means that I owe you, but it has been so damn long that I wont pay you. A very unjust law, and the sun of a gun that got it up, ought to have been hanged before it Ever became a law. Thats my "opin."

Well I was dead broke and highly insulted. I had been working for wages then about 3 years. The first time that I had went to work for wages was in 1886. A man by the name of Tom Allen had a Government Contract to deliver 1,600 head of Heifer Yearlings at San Carlos & Fort a Pachy Ariz.[12] He got me to ship the Cattle out there and

[12] Fort Apache, Arizona.

to get them to those two places. He went on ahead and had a Mormon outfit to meet me at Bowie Station, Ariz. There wasn't anything there but a few soldiers and a Depot, so we opened the doors and jumped those yearlings out of the cars.

We had a 40 mile drive to the Gila River without water. That was the time when the Government was chasing old Geronimo all over Hell & part of Ariz. trying to catch Him. All that was bothering me right at that time was that me and those mormons might beat the Government to the job. But we didn't, so we carried the herd down the River to San Carlos and delivered 1,000 head there, then carried the other 600 over to Ft. aPachy and delivered them. I guess that I saw every Indian that was in the tribe with the Exception of about 80 which was out on the war path with old Geronimo.

We had lots of fun while delivering those yearlings. Those Indians were not like any other tribes I Ever saw, and I had seen Indians all my life. They were all divided up in little squads, from 10 up to 90. Each of those little squads had a captain, and the Government gave Each Captain two head and Each Buck that was in the squad one head. There was a big long chute at the Pens where we pened the cattle, and we would fill that chute. The agent was a big fellow and one Eyed, but a bully fellow. We would tie a rope around the hind legs of the yearlings, and the Agent would make those old Buck Indians drag them back out and hold them down while He would

brand them. I put I C on all of them. But each squad had another brand to be put on too.

Of course these Indians didn't Know where to catch hold of a yearling to hold it down. They were just as apt to catch hold of one part as another, and yearlings big, fat, and wild. They just Kicked Hell out of those red Devils. The old agt. would hollow at them and curse them and they would jump on them yearlings like a bull tarrier. By the time they had began to learn how to hold a yearling down, that squad would be through. Then they would start off with them, and of course those year-lings was scared to death of them Indians and would run like the Devil. And when one Yearling run off by its self, all the Indians would quit the Bunch and take after that one yearling.

The Government was Keeping all those Indians there on the Reservation, learning them to farm. The Govern-ment had about 400 hired as scouts, paid them $20.00 per month in gold. That agt. told me that when He wanted one of those other Indians brought in for to be punished for something that He had done, all He had to say to the scouts was to get Him but not get hurt. He said that they would bring Him dead sometimes, but they would bring Him all the same, no matter whether He was their dady, brother, or who.

After the delivery of those yearlings I went back to Ft Worth. Then I got a letter from a man that had a Ranch in west of Abilene Tex. and wanted me to carry a lot of His Cattle to what was then called Greer Co. Tex. but now Oklahoma. 1886 was the dryest year that I have ever seen in Tex. and I have seen some pretty dry ones during my stay of about 50 years. So I went and taken the herd. There was about 2,250 head in this herd. They classed all the way up from a doggy calf[13] to a 6 or 7 year old beef steer. It was a hard drive to make on account of it being so awfully dry and the cattle was poor.

We crossed Red River at Doan's store and turned up the river to what was then called Tin City. There was a little store there mostly built out of tin cans, so that was the reason why it was christened Tin City, but afterwards

[13] Dogie—a motherless calf.

called Mangrum (or some such name).[14] There we left the river and drove over on a creek called Elm, which was only about 10 miles from Red River. There we turned the herd loose, and I taken the outfit back to get another herd of about 1,700 cattle and I drove them as far as Bitter Creek, which was after crossing Red River again at Doans store.

I had to be at court back in the lower country and couldn't go any farther with the herd. Being that the hard drive was behind us, I turned the outfit over to One of my Best men to take the herd on through, which would only take a few days to land them on Elm Creek where we had turned the other herd loose. So I saddled up a good horse, and like the fellows fool hunting dog, taken to the Back Trail.

There was another man ranching near Abilene that had a lot of cattle, which he wanted to move west, out near Odesa on the T & P R-R- so I helped gather a herd of about 1,600 head, and I drove them out to where I turned them loose on what is called Lunby's Draw, about 6 miles south of Odesa. I left a few of the Boys to look after the Cattle and went back after another herd. But I want to tell you before I tell you anything more, that we sure did have a bad storm while driving that first herd.

The storm struck us at what was called Rattle Snake Gap, about 12 or 15 miles west of what is called Big Springs. We all sure did put in a bad night, for it snowed, blowed, & froze, and those old cows drifted about 1½

---

[14] Mangum, seat of Greer County, Oklahoma.

miles with us, but we held them. This was the night of the 16th of Nov. which was another one of my happy Birth Days. I cant say that I liked this stormy month for Birth Days. But being that I had no say coming to me about what month my Birth Day should come in, so I had to accept the month Nov, so thats that.

We gathered another herd of about 700 head and drove them through to where we turned the other herd loose, got through after Xmas. After that Birth Day storm, it never did warm up any more that winter. I stood the last gard on both trips and we hadn't any watch, had only three gards, and I was supposed to go on at about three in the morning. But I know that it wasn't more than One lots of times. Those nights was sure cold and long. The North wind that was sweeping across those Plains didn't hesitate to ask you what you had done with your last summer's wages.

Well I stayed out there with the cattle the rest of that winter. You may have noticed by now that I haven't told you anything about what I was doing the year 1885. I dont aim to. I am like most Every other fellow that is keeping a diary, just have to forget a lot. But anyway I will say that I had another Birth Day.

The next spring I got a blur from a man that had about 6,000 head of Cattle over Northwest of Abilene about 50 or 60 miles, and the fall before He had moved a big lot of His cattle over on other peoples Range which He had no business to do. And He told them that He had leased up a big lot of that part of the Country, which was a lie. They soon found out that He had lied to them and had trespassed on their free Range. The most of the Country was being used at that time by the Ranch men without paying for anything.

The country was open Country at that time, and during the winters, cattle scattered badly and drifted a long ways from Home. When the spring round ups Came, men would send their Cow Boys in Every part of the Country to work. It was the custom of the Country to look out for Every Neighbor's Cattle and bring them in as near Home as they could. So all the Cow men had got togather and had organized against this fellow that had trespassed on them. They all had agreed among themselves to not let any of this fellow's men work with their wagons and not to allow any of their men to drive any of His cattle. So that left Him in a Hell of a fix, about 6,000 cattle and no good Neighbors.

I have seen fellows try to get along on the open Range independently, but they always made a failure of it. So I was the first one that He thought of, Knowing that I had lived and worked among all those other fellows for a number of years and was well liked and respected by all of them, from the cook up to the owners. He made a trade with me to take charge of His outfit for 8 months. I went back there about three weeks before the spring roundups started out and taken charge of His outfit. He had good horses and good Cow Boys too.

Those other fellows heard that I had come back there to run this fellow's outfit, and they came to see me to find out the straight of the business. They were all good true friends of mine, and I told them, yes that I aimed to gather this man's Cattle back to His own range.

They said, Well we had rather of seen any other man in the world come to take that job, than to have seen you take it, for we wanted to learn Him something.

I said, Well Boys, I know just how you all feel about it, and I think you have a right to feel that way, too. But I am broke and have to work for the Ones that will pay me the best wages. Although I hate to but in here, but I have taken the job and I am just the same fellow that I used to be when I lived here among you all, only I am broke.

Now I have this to say to you all, and it is this, that I am going to run a good clean outfit just as I used to here. And if you dont want me and my men to drive your cattle towards your Ranches, you will have to tell me not to, for I will instruct all my outside men to look after our Neighbors Cattle and bring them in just the same as if they were our own, and will appreciate the same favors.

There was not a Blooming one of them said to leave theirs. Everything was just like it always had been before the trouble. I stayed my contract out (8 months).

That winter I went to work for a man that had taken over 15,000 head of cattle right in the same part of the country, (the Salt Fork of the Brazos River). The men that had went broke, had not been able to pay off all their men and owed some of their Cow Boys quite a little sum of money. Of course no big sum, but enough that they wanted it pretty bad. All those cattle covered a good big country. There was a lot of those Boys that felt pretty sore because they couldn't collect their wages that was due them. There was quite a few of those Boys that had a brand of their own, and some that didn't soon had. I was to take a wagon and about 3 men and just drift around over the Range and brand all the Calves that had been missed on the round ups. Well a lot of those Boys was doing some pretty "dirty work," such as killing cows for their calves and branding big calves that they thought would not be seen, before they were weaned. There was several brands started that no one ever claimed. I bared brands on calves that was following their mothers which belong to my outfit, and those that wasn't following I left alone, although there was a good many that I was satisfied belong to my outfit. That was the winter of 87 & 88 (or 88 I might say).

The next spring, this outfit wanted me to cut the Trail[15] for them, (or for Him rather) as it belonged only to one man. So I went up the Brazos near Seamore[16] and cut Trail herds for about six weeks. Then I went back to the Ranch, and in about two weeks I quit.

There was a fellow that had about 300 head of horses, and He was getting ready to leave the country. Said that He was going to Washington Territory and wanted me to go with Him. I told him, "Star Bueno."[17] His camp

[15] Gather herds to be driven up the trail.
[16] Seymour, Texas, seat of Baylor County.
[17] *Está bueno* ("It is well," or "OK"). Another jocular form is "Star wainer."

106

was on a creek called Big Stinking creek. Not a very nice
Name do you think? Well it was nice enough for the
water that was in it.

So I rode half broke, whole broke, and some not broke
atal, that was the kind of horses we had to ride, in gathering those horses.

I got a fall one day and broke my collar bone. I believe that is the name it is called by. Anyway it was a
bone damn close to my neck, just a little too close to feel

good. That whole country was a solid prairie dog town, and in running along in "high" one day, my old digger ramed his foot down a dog hole, and we stopped in low.

There was three other fellows with me. They made a ball out of my vest and put it under my arm, tied my arm against my body and tied a grass hopple[18] to my rist and around my neck. (Some skill, no?) I didn't know beans from dried apples for about an hour and a half, but we was all going to camp. They had put me on a gentle horse. Mine was only about half broke, and I was about whole broke in more ways than one.

In a few days I was up and going again with my arm in a sling. So we got those old "yeyua's"[19] togather and pulled North. We got as far as Tascosa on the Canadian River, and I hopped the cut.[20]

I went to work for the XIT outfit.[21] They had about 100,000 head of cattle, at least was what they claimed. I worked there a couple of months, then went back to Tascosa, stayed there about a week, then went on down the road to Clarington.

There I got a job running a ranch.

[18] Hobble.

[19] Colloquial variant of Spanish *yeguas*, "mares."

[20] Left the group. When a cow breaks out of the herd into which she has been driven, she has "hopped the cut."

[21] The XIT Ranch, one of the largest ranches in the United States, is in the Texas Panhandle, north of Amarillo.

Wells and Barbed Wire

THIS WAS THE FALL of 1888. It was not a very big ranch,[1] only about 4,000 head of cattle. I worked on that Ranch until the spring of 1890, and the man that owned it swapped it off for a ranch on the Colorado River, 20 miles south of Colorado City, Tex., so I had to move all those cattle down to that Ranch, which I taken in two herds.

I stayed on that Ranch until the next spring, then I quit. The man that owned the Ranch lived in DeKalb, Ill., and He had the wrong ideas about some things, from my way of thinking. For that reason, I quit. He was a fine man and awful wealthy. He didn't want me to quit,

[1] A ranch owned by R. L. Elwood in Donley County, in the Texas Panhandle. (*The New Encyclopedia of Texas* [Texas Development Bureau, Dallas, n.d.], Vol. IV, p. 71.)

but I did. When He settled up with me, He gave me $500.00 more than was due me on my wages. So I call that kind of a man a real "Gem."

That spring, another fellow that owned a paster joining this Ranch, and I kinder threw in together and built a house, dug a well etc. He had no money and no stock, had went broke, so I had a little money and I financed our business. He taken in a lot of cattle to pasture, and we put a nice lot of improvements on the Place, and I stayed there until fall.

Then Mr. H. K. Thurber the big wholesale man of N.Y. City, and also the owner of the coal mines (Thurber)[2] sent me out to a Ranch He owned, 75 miles west of Roswell, N.M. The Ranch is Known as the three Block Ranch. He wanted me to cut a herd of Beef that was being gathered to be shipped down near His coal mine (Thurber's). I was out there two weeks and I had orders when I got through cutting this Beef herd to come to Ft. Worth, where Mr. Thurber's manager lived, old Col. Hunter, who used to be one of the well known Commission Co.[3] of Hunter & Evans of St. Louis. So I went to Ft. Worth, and I was sent to the Big Horse Ranch 14 miles North of

[2] Now a ghost town with only a few families, Thurber, Texas, had about 10,000 inhabitants when it was the center of the coal-mining operations in the northwestern corner of Erath County. Established in 1886 as a mining camp by the Johnson Coal Company, it was named Thurber in 1888 when ownership passed to the Texas Pacific Coal and Gas Company. (Mary Jane Gentry, "Thurber, Texas," *The Handbook of Texas* [Texas State Historical Association, Austin, Tex., 1952], Vol. I, p. 779.)

[3] The cowman's middleman. The commission company usually operates at the stockyard, buying from the cattle-grower and selling to the feeder or packer.

Cheyenne City, Wyo., belonging to the Big Coffee men, Arbuckle, Jones, & H. K. Thurber.[4]

I had orders to select 5 car loads of the best mares that could be rounded up on the Ranch and two of the best imported stallions out of about 60 head, which was on the Ranch, and to bring them back to Mr. Thurber's Ranch, which was not over 12 or 15 miles from the Town of Thurber. He had about 10,000 acres in a pasture there, so I was told, but I didn't go to it when I brought the mares down. After I got through with the mares, I went back to where I called Home.

It was getting along towards winter by that time, so I dened up until about the first of Feb. when I got a letter from a man living in Sherman Tex. asking me to go to Alpine Tex. and take charge of a Ranch.[5] It was a incorporated company, a bunch of Boston Guys. So I went and taken charge of the outfit. It wasn't a big Ranch, only about 3,000 head of cattle. The co. had been leasing land for about 10 years, and they owned 24,000 Acres over East of the Pecos River that was being used by other people, (free of all charges). The man that sent me to take charge of the Ranch, had a couple of wells drilled on this land East of the Pecos and told me to move to it.

[4] Despite the discrepancy in initials, the reference may be to Francis Beatty Thurber (1842–1907), a successful wholesale grocer and author of *Coffee from Plantation to Cup* (1878). (*Who Was Who in America, 1897–1942* [The A. N. Marquis Co., Chicago, 1942], p. 1238.)

[5] According to *The New Encyclopedia of Texas*, Carpenter went to work for the Hereford Cattle Company at Alpine, Texas, about 1894 or 1895, having previously, in 1891, "re-entered the cattle business for himself in Sterling County, forming a partnership with John S. McWilliams that lasted three or four years." (Vol. IV, p. 71.)

The fall of 1892 during Xmas week, I pulled out with about 1,760 head. We had all Kinds of bad weather during the time we was gathering those cattle. It was about 10 miles south of Alpine in the mountains, and it was trying to storm and do Everything Else but something nice. The fog would be so thick of nights that we couldn't see the cattle, and they would just walk off from 7 or 8 men on gard. We lost the herd 3 different nights before we got off with them. You see it was right in their Range and they wanted to get away and did.

At the wind-up it snowed and cleared off, leaving about 2½ inches of snow on the ground. It was pretty cold sailing. We crossed the S-P-R-R-[6] about 4 miles east of Alpine, Xmas Eve. Ft. Stockton was on the route, a distance of about 40 miles, if I am not mistaken. When we got within about 12 miles of Stockton, one Evening pretty late, it began to rain and in a short time the rain turned to snow, so we struck Camp. We had two wagons, one being a Corn wagon, for we had to feed our horses. We beded the herd up against the south side of a Hill, called the 12 mile Hill. It wasn't much of a wind break, but it was the best in sight.

Those cattle walked & troted until three O'Clock in the morning. They would walk up hill & trot down hill. We all was around the herd, and there was plenty of sotol[7] so we built fires all around the herd. Guess we must

6 The Southern Pacific Railroad.
7 A palmlike cactus that usually grows to six or seven feet in height and about one and one-half feet in trunk diameter. The long, narrow leaves

of had as many as a dozen fires or more, and we would leave our horses standing at the fires and take it afoot. About 3 O'Clock in the morning it quit snowing & went to freezing, then the cattle layed down. I sent all of the men to the wagon to go to bed but myself and another man.

The next morning we left 6 head of Cattle on the bed ground, being too near dead to get up. But oh, suffering snakes, wasn't it cold!

It cleared off nice but not warm, so it was cold all the rest of the trip. We moved on down the Draw about 20 miles from Stockton at a place called China Ponds. That was our last water until we struck the Pecos River a distance of about 40 miles East. We watered good One Evening and then pulled out East and made a good Evening drive and Camped, grazed the Cattle good and beded them down about dark, ate our suppers, caught night horses as usual, and all hit the hay but for the first gard. Put the horse rangler to gard the horses, for we did not hopple them that night.

The moon Came up about 11 O'Clock and we rolled again for the Pecos. We drove the rest of that night and stopped at daylight, got breakfast, changed horses, grazed our Cattle a Couple of hours, and pulled out again. We got to the Pecos that Evening. We hit the river, and the Cattle was dry and went partly in to drink.

It was a nice place to Cross, no bank on the far side, just a nice sand bar on both sides, so we pushed the cattle

---

produced remain on the trunk after they die and make a roaring blaze when the trunk is set on fire.

up and tried to force them on across the river to the far side. But we could not get them to lead out. It was swift but not over Belly deep to a Cow and not over 60 yds. wide. We worked for an hour or so trying to Cross them. We would rope calves and drag them across, and their mothers would follow over after them. And we would tie the calf over there and go back and get another one and do the same way. I think at One time we had about half. doz. tied on the opposite side from the herd, but damn them, they would not go across.

We drove our Cows & Calves back to the herd and throwed the herd back about a quarter of a mile or more and let them graze until night, then beded them down for the night. You see those Cattle had been raised in those mountains south of Alpine, and the bigest water they had Ever seen was a spring, only when a big rain happened along, which wasn't very often. So they was afraid of so much water.

The next morning we throwed them off of the bed ground and grazed them good for about 2 hours and put the horses in with them and drove them down to the river again, and got the horses, which was about 45 head, to lead out across. But Devil Cow that would go. We tried Everything that we could think of, but no use, they would not Cross.

We drove them back out to graze again, and after dinner I moved the Camp up close to the River, so it would be handy for the night gards. We was out of grub almost, really was out of several things that we need, and

we was all as full of "gray backs"[8] as any mexican that
Ever crossed the Rio Grande. We had a mexican or two
along, and I never doubted but what they had divided up
with the rest of the outfit. Anyway we had them, and
plenty at that.

We Killed a beef that night and beded the Cattle on
the sand bar at the Crossing, just as close to the river as
we could get them. I told the Boys that If they never did
Cross, that we would have their bones all close togather

[8] Body lice.

so that the bone haulers[9] would not have any trouble loading their wagons.

Next morning about sun up, they walked across. We wasn't over about three days drive to where we was going, so we got there and turned loose on the 18 day of Jan. 1893.

I sent the men all back to Alpine where they belong, only a Couple of them, so they had to take the wagon along, as it was about 200 miles. I kept the Negro cook with me. Had one man to take His mount of horses with Him as to look after our reminent of Cattle and told another one of the Boys, which didn't belong at Alpine, to bring the wagon back, which He did and then went on up about Colorado City where He belonged. So me and the cook held the Camp down the rest of the winter.

During the winter our cattle had scattered all over the Country, it being all open range at that time. Lots of our Cattle had fevered pretty badly, for they had come out of a high country where there was no ticks, so lots of them had died too. To cap things off about right, the fellow that lived in Sherman Tex. that was trying to "ram rod" the outfit, turn in and sold all the Cattle that my man had already gathered on the Alpine Ranch at a very low price, (there was over 300 head) and sold all the reminent that Could be found in adjacent Country.

Well Pecos Co. joined Bruster,[10] and the Pecos River

[9] Roving waggoners who collected and sold bones of buffalo and other animals.

[10] Brewster County, Texas, of which Alpine is the county seat.

was all that lay between Pecos & Crocket Co. I had turned loose in Crocket. The simple fact was that those Alpine men that had bought the reminent got lots of Cattle that drifted back across the Pecos. I had men out on the round ups Everywhere but never the less I was out lots of Cattle when fall came, and we had a bad drought that year too. That was the summer of 1893.

During all this time, The Treasure of this Company bought out all those other Boston "Guys" and turned the whole "smear" over to me to run to suit myself, and He would foot all the bills until we Could get Expense money out of the Cattle. I flew at it, fenced the ranch, put down more wells, bought more land, and Block lands[11] with some of my joining Neighbors. So I Come right up. I handled the ranch just the same as if I owned it and had no poor Kin. The old man that really did own it, would come down about Once a year.

After 2 or 3 years, He let me take the Ranch for 3 years on the Shares. I got along alright. When the 3 years was up, I turned the old man His Ranch back, which then consisted of 84 sections of land and a big herd of Cattle, which He sold and quit the Texas Ranch business for good. He was running a large Dining Room in Boston.

I moved across the Pecos River[12] with about 1,500

[11] Blocked lands, that is, traded acreage with adjoining neighbors so as to straighten the property lines.

[12] Apparently Carpenter's move here is from Pecos County, eastward across the Pecos River to Crockett County. According to *The New Encyclopedia of Texas*, "In 1900 he moved to Pecos County and shortly afterward to Terrell County, where he established his present ranch," which was "twelve miles north of Dryden on the Sheffield Road." (Vol. IV, p. 71.)

head of Cattle, about 20 head of good saddle horses and two or three thousand dollars in Cash and started me a Ranch. It was all open Range where I moved to, and my Cattle scattered all over the Country the same as Everybody Else's did. We had drought on top of drought, and Cattle went down to a "mere song." And other misfortunes Come my way, so after about 6 years of "life on the Pecos," I sold all my Cattle and Ranch too. It was the spring of 1900 that I moved on the west side of the Pecos.

After selling out, I started me another Ranch, but not on the Pecos, about 30 miles to the west of it. After delivering my Cattle, which taken all the summer, and having a deep well drilled and build me a good House, and puting other improvements on my new Ranch, I had about $2,700.00 to the good, 250 head of goats, and about 30 head of stock horses. I taken the $2,700.00 and put it all into more goats. I still had a pretty good little reminent of Cattle scattered up & down the Pecos River. I guess I did get as much as $3,000.00 out of that reminent.

Right here I leave off with "My Diary," for I think when an old cow man that has spent the best part of His life handleing Cattle, quits the Cattle business and goes to herding goats, that it is high time that He should quit Keeping tabs on His Self. And furthermore when old women bob their hair to run for Governor of the state of Texas. But the K-K-K-'s[13] will have to admit they found

[13] The reference is to Miriam A. Ferguson, governor of Texas, 1925–27, 1933–35. During Mrs. Ferguson's first campaign in 1924, it was said that she was supported by the Ku Klux Klan. The metaphor is mixed with a reference to tuning a model-T motor for all kinds of weather.

"Ma" in perfect running order and well adjusted, (to heat and cold).

As I have given a pretty clear and accurate account of My "Young life" without any exaggeration as my memory will permit, while I have left out quite a number of incidents that happened in my "old life," which would perhaps not prove as interesting to others as they did to me. Morally, I will say that I am about on a par with my fellow man. And as to honesty, will say that I have only stolen, from a citron up to a pretty woman, which the latter proved a "Jonah." So being past the danger age, I have no fears, and right here, I leave it all up to the Bobbed hair & the autos.

"Au revoir."

PS/

Being this much like a woman, I want to add this to my Diary, and it is this, That I owe myself a apology for not Knowing that I was agoing to live so long, for if I had Known, I certainly would have been a preacher. There's 2 things I never have seen, a dead gray mule & a dead preacher.

LUCKY 7

A Cowman's Autobiography

HAS BEEN SET IN ELEVEN-POINT WAVERLEY TYPE

WITH FOUR POINTS OF LEADING

PRINTED LETTERPRESS ON SIXTY-POUND WARREN'S

OLDE STYLE ANTIQUE WOVE PAPER

AND BOUND IN DUPONT CRAFTSMAN BINDING CLOTH

BY THE UNIVERSITY OF TEXAS

PRINTING DIVISION

FOR THE

University of Texas Press